First Aid Kit for the Mind ...
Lovely in its presentatic
personal stories; essenti
way at patterns and trig;
wonderful teacher and f
and creativity. – **Martin**
and author of *Let Go: A Buddhist Guide to Breaking Free of Habits*

Vimalasara Mason-John's *First Aid Kit for the Mind: Breaking the Cycle of Habitual Behaviors* does a marvelous job of explaining how we all develop intricate habits that ultimately limit us, but from which we can break free with the right tools. The author draws from her own backstory to present a compassionate and practical approach to overcoming behaviors that keep us from living our best lives.

But it's not a collection of quick fixes; it delves deep into the roots of habits, exploring the underlying causes and providing insight and strategies for great change. Vimalasara's approach is holistic and accessible, blending mindfulness practices, cognitive-behavioral techniques, and ancient wisdom traditions in a way that can be easily digested and applied.

First Aid Kit for the Mind is a masterclass that will leave a lasting impact on any reader seeking to transform their relationship with themselves. I wholeheartedly recommend this book to anyone ready to embark on a life-changing journey of self-discovery and self-improvement. – **Stephen Berkley**, filmmaker, TEDx speaker

Every household needs this first aid kit! Vimalasara takes an unflinching look at where it hurts and offers essential supplies for healing. This book packs a lot of ancient wisdom into a small space, along with clear instructions that anyone can use. Only trustworthy, good stuff here. Highly recommended for life! – **Christopher Germer**, Ph.D., Lecturer, Department of Psychiatry, Harvard Medical School, author of *The Mindful Path to Self-Compassion*

First Aid Kit for the Mind is a remarkably concise guide to dealing with the most difficult mind/body states. Vimalasara has a gift for capturing the essence of the problem and giving us the exact help we need for healing. This is the most directly practical set of tools for dealing with addiction and underlying trauma I've ever read. – **Kevin Griffin**, author of *One Breath at a Time: Buddhism and the Twelve Steps* and *Living Kindness: Metta Practice for the Whole of Our Lives*

As a clinician, educator, and trainer, this inspiring and insightful book left me in absolute awe of Mason-John's wisdom and guidance as one of the premier social, cultural, and psychological healers of our time. I can't imagine anyone reading this book, whether client, student, practitioner, or casual reader, without feeling a sense of personal empowerment, enhanced insight, and a renewed will to break cycles of harmful and habitual behaviors. This book is a must-read! – **Kenneth V. Hardy**, Ph.D., author of *Racial Trauma: Clinical Strategies and Techniques for Healing Invisible Wounds* and editor of *The Enduring, Invisible, and Ubiquitous Centrality of Whiteness*

In this gem of a book Vimalasara distills eons of wisdom, many years of study, and decades of deep personal experience. The result is an entertaining, succinct, and highly practical primer to help us get through the many challenging moments life has a way of throwing at us. – **Gabor Maté, MD**, author of *The Myth of Normal: Trauma, Illness and Healing in a Toxic Culture*

Vimalasara's *First Aid Kit for the Mind* is a user-friendly guide for meeting our minds with kindness and compassion even when we're struggling the most. Their no-nonsense approach offers readers a chance for freedom from the myriad of habitual tendencies in which we often find ourselves stuck. – **Sharon Salzberg**, author of *Lovingkindness* and *Real Life*

Vimalasara's book is exactly the salve we need in this moment and time. In this work, Vimalasara allows us the opportunity to shift from overwhelming dread towards practices of healing and balance, creating more opportunities for accessing joy. Drawing from her ancestors and her compassionate way of being allows Vimalasara to offer strategies and tools that make this book accessible to everyone who is seeking to shift from ongoing stress or unwanted behaviors, to living more fully with the gifts life has to offer. You'll want to check it out! – **Fresh "Lev" White**, diversity trainer, speaker, spiritual leader, contributor to *Real World Mindfulness for Beginners*; *Transcending: Trans Buddhist Voices*; *Trans Bodies, Trans Selves*; and *Authentic Selves: Celebrating Trans and Nonbinary People and Their Families*

Vimalasara's writing is a clearly and beautifully articulated set of practices to use the power of the mind, but not to be controlled or be seduced by it. She speaks through lineages and generations into the equanimity and balance of heart-mind-body, which will benefit all of us. – **Larry Yang**, author of *Awakening Together: The Spiritual Practice of Inclusivity and Community*

VALERIE (VIMALASARA)
MASON-JOHN

FIRST
AID KIT
for the
MIND

Breaking the cycle of
habitual behaviors

Windhorse Publications
38 Newmarket Road
Cambridge CB5 8DT

info@windhorsepublications.com

windhorsepublications.com

llustrations, text design, and typesetting
by Francesca Romano Design

British Library Cataloguing in Publication Data:

A catalogue record for this book is available
from the British Library.

ISBN 978-1-915342-23-2

CONTENTS

About the author

Valerie (Vimalasara) Mason-John has worked as an international correspondent covering Aboriginal deaths in custody, and interviewed Sinn Fein prisoners and ex-rebels from the Sierra Leone war. Their work in the field of conflict transitioned into working with gangs, the incarcerated, bullies, and challenging behavior. Valerie is equipped to work in many modalities. A teacher in the Triratna Buddhist Community, a mindfulness trainer, and a founding facilitator of Dr. Gabor Maté's Compassionate Inquiry, they have also trained in Internal Family Systems, Embodied Somatics, Breathworks, and Shamanism. Their ten books include *Detox Your Heart: Meditations for Emotional Trauma, Eight Step Recovery: Using the Buddha's Teachings to Overcome Addiction,* and more recently *I'm Still Your Negro: An Homage to James Baldwin*. They work as an international public speaker and trainer in the field of mindfulness for trauma and addiction, and interview high-profile Buddhist and spiritual teachers and leaders for the Wisdom for Life platform. Valerie/Vimalasara has a private counseling/healing practice and lives in Canada with their partner.

Acknowledgments

I am my ancestors' wildest dream. The fact that I have a
certain amount of freedom as a person living in a black,
female, queer, gender-fluid body in the West would have
been unthinkable for my parents' generation. I thank
the ancestors for imparting their wisdom to me. Their
teachings come through me. The ideas that I share in
the book have been taught for thousands of years.
I thank my root teacher, Buddha Shakyamuni, who
rediscovered the way. I thank my late teachers the
venerable Sangharakshita and Thich Nhat Hanh for
making the wisdom teachings accessible to me. Thank
you to my private preceptor Ratnavandna, for gifting
me with my name. I have recently been influenced by
my teacher friends Dr. Gabor Maté and Arisika Razak,
and my supportive and affirming partner Che Kehoe.
Thank you to my dear friend Nina Rapi for being a
reader and giving me helpful feedback. Thank you to
Manidha who asked me, "Well if it's a first aid kit for the
mind, where is the Band-Aid, the bandage?" Thank you
to Viveka for her generosity and to Liz Mars for helping
me make some creative decisions. Thank you to Jenica
for her positive joyful heart. Thank you to Marvin Paul
Regier for his attention to detail while recording all my
meditations. Always thank you to my plentiful friends
who make sure I have some fun, laughter, and joy in

my life. Thank you to Dhammamegha, who could see the potential in a course that I had developed, and with her constructive feedback found a new book for me to write. This book would not be possible without the collaboration of the Windhorse team; special thanks to Michelle Bernard, Francesca Romano, and Walter Monticelli. Thank you to all of you who will take the time to read all or some of the book. And thank you to all of you who have supported my work throughout the years.

Publisher's acknowledgments

We would like to thank the patrons who gave generously and anonymously to support the production of this book. One of these donations was made in appreciation of the life of Dharmacharini Vijayatara.

And we also thank the individuals who donated through our "Sponsor-a-book" campaign. You can find out more about it at https://www.windhorsepublications.com/ sponsor-a-book/.

Windhorse Publications wish to gratefully acknowledge a grant from the Future Dharma Fund and the Triratna European Chairs' Assembly Fund toward the production of this book.

Audio recordings

First Aid Kit for the Mind has been produced with accompanying guided meditations by the author.

They are indicated by this image

These can be streamed directly from the web.

Please go to https://www.windhorsepublications.com/ free-resources/fakftm-audio/

> *Your true nature is open
> and free, but you cover it up.*

NISARGADATTA MAHARAJ

*As a child I loved the job of polishing brass
cutlery. I would rub and rub for hours and then,
from nowhere, the bright gleam would appear
just like a beautiful jewel. Our mind/heart needs
polishing too. Our conditioning, our tendencies,
the biases we accumulate throughout life
cover up the beauty of the mind/heart. May this
pocketbook help to rub away the muck
we have collected over the years so that,
from nowhere, the bright gleam might appear,
reflecting our true essence.*

Why this pocketbook is for you

While coming to the completion of this book, the question arose: *Who am I writing this for?* As writers, often we don't just write for an audience, we also write for ourselves. And when writing a book for self-development, self-healing, I have to ask myself, *Do these ideas really work? Am I walking my talk?* To be transparent, yes – I know these tips and ideas do help to break the habitual cycles because I am proof of that. And yet, there are still some habits that I work with, like my attachment to raw cashew nuts. When I am practicing these skills in this book, there is no attachment to them; when I'm not paying attention to my own teachings, the raw cashew nuts become a nuisance in my life. So yes, you can break habits if you commit to practice.

I have taught much of what I have written here to both adults and young people at risk, young people who are labeled as having challenging behavior, young people who have been incarcerated. I remember taking a group of schoolchildren on a team building weekend, which involved many trust exercises including high ropes activity. I remember turning to a colleague and saying, "That kid up there is going to kill someone;

we have to bring them down – they are still habitually bullying." We brought the child down and, for the rest of the weekend, we could not allow them to do anything that might have put another child or themselves at risk. I had the conversation with them. Told them that, if they began incorporating some of the skills we had taught them, began to become aware of their triggers, feelings, and thoughts, they would be able to achieve great things. Eight years later, I opened up Messenger on Facebook, and in my inbox was this kid who said, "I'm so glad I found you. I want to tell you I have begun integrating all the things you taught me back then, and I am achieving great things." What an endorsement. So yes, young people can benefit from this book too.

As my reflection goes deeper, I feel the spirit of the many black people who have been shot dead by the police because they answered back or did not do what the police demanded, or simply because they were black, Hispanic, Latinx. It rattles my nervous system because I know that could have been me.

When I was fifteen, on an anti-Nazi march, carrying a banner, the police singled me out among my white peers and asked for my banner. Completely activated, I said, "Why are you picking on me, what about all the white people?" Still holding on to my banner, not able to finish my next sentence, I was arrested, handcuffed, and thrown into a police van. I was driven to a police cell and asked if I had dangerous weapons, and then a policewoman rammed her hand up inside me. If I had known what I know now, I would have sensed in my body a pounding when the police officer came up to me, caught myself going into an unhelpful story – *this is racism*. Unhelpful because, while it may well have been racism, the story of racism in that moment completely consumed my mind, put me into fight mode, and I was unable to just hand the banner over. It could have saved me from sexual assault.

I know these tools can't do anything about the body I've been born into or chosen to inhabit, but they can help save my life if I realize I have been completely activated or triggered – if I can take a pause so I don't end up in a police cell or dead.

I have lost it several times at airports, and have been lucky that I've not been shot at and killed, like the Polish immigrant Robert Dziekanski who displayed frustration and agitation with airport staff at my local airport in Vancouver in 2007. Today, before I travel, I use some of these tools to help me break my habitual trauma response to fight when activated by racism, sexism, homophobia.

So I hope some of these tools will help to save a life. We know that alcoholism, drug addiction, and many other forms of addictive behaviors can be a matter of life and death. We know that being completely obsessed with surfing on the internet or scrolling on a cell phone can result in people forgetting to pick children up from school and other important commitments.

And I hope this book will speak to people who just want to be happier, who are looking for more stillness, simplicity, and contentment in their lives.

You don't need to identify as someone with addictions – you just need to identify with being human. After all, who doesn't have unhealthy habits? Habits can be helpful, but some aren't. This book focuses on the habits you want to change, and the vicious cycle of habits you may want to interrupt and break.

All of us have experienced trauma of some kind. The one trauma we all share is birth, and we spend the rest of our life making sense of the experience in the womb and outside of the womb. Some people, however, have a truckload of trauma and are still living within it. For those of you in the middle of a traumatic crisis, the best thing, alongside reading this book, is to find someone who will attune to you and listen without judgment.

This book can be read like a course. Take your time, check in with someone. It does not have to be linear either. You can open the book, as you would dip into a pack of cards, and see which page you land on. These teachings are for anybody who is ready to receive them.

Be aware of your body posture while reading the pocketbook. If you notice your body is slumped or hunched over, open the body up, becoming aware of the length of your body as well as the width and your center. Take up space with dignity. A slouched body can express a sense of being defeated. Can you sit with sadness in an upright position and know these feelings are welcome and normal? Give yourself a chance – open up the body, have a sense of expansiveness to help cultivate confidence and shift stress and tension. It's well known that the position of our body impacts sensations, thoughts, feelings, emotions, perceptions, and much more. Mind and body are not separate: they influence each other. The tensions we carry in our body, how we hold our body, are often a physical expression of our mental states. I invite you to sit, stand, or lie down tall, experiencing the length and width of your whole being, with your body open as an invitation to saying yes to these teachings.

No mind, never mind,
where is the mind?

1

WHY A FIRST AID KIT FOR THE MIND?

There is so much suffering in the world, so much trauma in the world, that humans have always explored ways to help soothe the living organism of the body, where our feelings, emotions, thoughts, and physical activity occur throughout our life. We have a first aid kit specifically for the body when it has succumbed to a trauma. It makes sense that we should have one for the mind, which also experiences trauma.

Perhaps the biggest trauma that the mind can experience is our tendency to see the mind and heart as separate. If we began looking for the mind, we would most probably point to the head. But, upon exploration, we would find that the mind is everywhere in the body. It's most definitely not separate from the body or indeed the heart.

Buddhist psychology uses one word – *citta* – to describe the mind and heart, and *citta* includes both the rational mind and the feeling mind. It's the doorway to compassion.

Trauma arises when the mind and heart disconnect, leading to a profound rupture in our emotional landscape. We have learned to push the heart out of our mind, leaving us with just rational thoughts that can torment us. For the mind to heal, it needs to embrace the heart with breath and compassion. We push the heart out by not breathing deeply, and by holding on to our breath. There is so much scientific research proving the benefits of breathing deeply and working with the breath. People over the past ten years have been inspired by the Wim Hof method of breathing, which teaches us to inhale deeply and exhale without forcing the breath out, and there has been a plethora of training programs teaching people breathing techniques like pranayama, holotropic, or box breathing. Our breath is medicine.

We know that when the brain doesn't get enough oxygen, it causes brain damage. Every time we get angry, act out of resentment, or get out of control with an emotion, it's almost like having temporary brain damage. Our breathing becomes restricted, we take shorter in-breaths, and this impacts the brain. Early signs of oxygen deprivation can be a change in heart rate, being unable to think clearly, seeing spots, an inability to follow directions, decreased judgment or awareness, seizures.

Take a moment and clench your fists really, really tight, and you may notice that you are holding your breath. This is what can happen when we are activated: we tighten up and stop breathing at full capacity.

When you become angry, frustrated, enraged, does this sound familiar? One or more of the above are also signs that we have lost control of our emotions. And, while we may not need to call emergency services, we do need a first aid kit. The good news is that the first aid kit for the mind doesn't cost anything. It's with us all the time.

The first aid kit will offer a healing possibility and create a necessary pause so we can begin the deeper work. The kit can be used as a healing aid to help stop the noisy traffic and the pileup of thoughts that often crash the mind. Just as a Band-Aid can help stop the flow of blood, there are many items in the first aid kit to help stop the flow of behaviors that may harm ourselves and/or others.

Ask yourself, *Do I exhibit recurring patterns of behavior?* Even if you don't perceive any of your behaviors to be compulsive, addictive, or habitual, still ask yourself, *Is there something I am doing that is causing me some misery in my life? Is there something I have been doing for years and have not been able to stop? Would I like to be happier in my life?* If you answer yes to any of these questions, then maybe this pocketbook is for you. Read it for yourself, rather than for someone else, and surrender to the process.

It's normal to experience some kind of activation (like strong emotional or mental states arising) when reading this book. Please reach out to somebody. Activation of emotions is just pointing to unresolved stuff in our lives.

One of the reasons we have strong habitual behaviors is because, in childhood, many of us had nobody to speak to, nobody to connect with. So we began speaking to ourselves, beating ourselves up. Some of us didn't have healthy adults to attach to, and, because attachment is so important, we began attaching first to our dolls, toys, or pets, and as we grew older to addictive and compulsive behaviors that gave us respite. These behaviors became our best friends. Our pets, addictions, and behaviors didn't let us down in the same way adults in our life did. Our habits and compulsive or addictive behaviors were more reliable, and predictable.

The first aid kit will help to develop what Dan Siegel, MD calls the "window of tolerance." It describes "the optimal zone of 'arousal' for a person to function in everyday life. When a person is operating within this zone or window, they can effectively manage and cope with their emotions."[1]

When we are able to spend time in the window of tolerance, we can function and thrive more, and relate to ourselves and others in a much healthier way. The amygdala in the brain begins to settle, stress levels go down, and we can begin to diffuse any situation of perceived threat.

What if the first aid kit doesn't work? Often the Band-Aid, the bandage, the pill is a temporary fix until we can get the help we need to take care of the trauma to the body. This kit will do the same, while also offering some practices to get to the root of things. You may need extra help, especially if you have experienced trauma of the mind/heart. Additional help can include a variety of therapeutic approaches, legal psychedelic-assisted therapies, plus shamanic ceremonies and rituals.

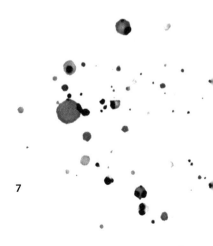

Watch your triggers; they become stories
Watch your stories; they become excuses
Watch your excuses; they become relapses
Watch your relapses; they become dis-eases
Watch your dis-eases; they become vicious cycles
Watch your vicious cycles; they become your wheel of life.

2

FREEDOM FROM OUR TRIGGERS

INSIDE THE KIT
Salve

When we are triggered, an old wound has been irritated – we need the touch of our own hand upon our body as the salve to soothe the old wound.

IN AN EMERGENCY
Yawn

It may seem ludicrous. My mime and physical theater teacher Desmond Jones used to say that a yawn is a silent scream. Yawning can activate a repair circuit that can trigger the parasympathetic nervous system, which in turn will calm everything down in the body. Try it – when the mind has been assailed by a trigger and you are in activation mode, you may want to shout, scream. A yawn is a great substitute, as you get to stretch the throat, and if you burst out laughing, so what. It's worked!

TIP

When you're triggered, ask yourself, *Who is pulling my trigger? Where is the trigger that is causing so much activation?* Ask yourself, *How familiar is this trigger? How old was I when I first experienced trigger activation?* When you are able to identify the age, know that this is often who is present when we are activated, and this young person who is present needs your attention. The adult in you will need to remind that young part of you that you are no longer young: you are an adult who will take care of it and have its back. Now place your hand upon your heart and take a yawn.

Let's delve deeper into what our triggers can look like

The dictionary describes a trigger as "a small device that releases a spring or catch and so sets off a mechanism, especially in order to fire a gun." Our body is sometimes like that gun. For example, when our triggers are pulled or our buttons are pushed, we can become explosive. Our stories, excuses, relapses, dis-eases, vicious cycles are the ammunition that can destroy our lives and those of others.

When we are triggered, an old wound has been activated. Our window of tolerance has narrowed, and we can be stuck in the fight or flight mode that Dan Siegel calls the sympathetic state, or we can be in the shutdown, disconnection mode that he calls the dorsal vagal state. We can begin to widen the window of tolerance and move into what Siegel calls the ventral stage: a place of connection and safety, accessible through the touch of our own hand upon our body. The warmth and touch of our own hand can be the salve to soothe the deep layered wounds that have been activated. Things that trigger us can be our greatest teacher, and sometimes our worst enemy.

Freedom

When we react from the place of a trigger, we have lost our equilibrium and our brain becomes befuddled and confused, sometimes expressing symptoms of a "temporary brain injury." The flow of breath is constricted, we tense up, we say and do things we wouldn't do when calm and relaxed. We write things in an email or a text message, for example, and later we regret doing so.

Freedom arises when we feel the ping of sensations caused by the triggers and we turn toward them without interpreting the sensations in the body, just letting sensations arise without making our feelings mean anything. When we habitually make meaning out of our feelings, out of other people's actions, we become the meaning making machines that churn out unhelpful interpretations and harmful stories.

What if I'm still triggered? If you notice you have been triggered, this is an excellent sign. More often we don't realize we have been activated until after we have reacted. When we are so much more aware of our body becoming activated, this means we can interrupt the energy of a trigger and pause. The pause interrupts the unconscious automatic reaction, enabling us with

the choice not to react from a place of an old story that
has been activated. Then we don't get seduced by the
vicious circles of our excuses, of acting out of anger,
or of relapsing into compulsive or adaptive behavior.

It's possible to have freedom from our triggers. It's
possible, when someone waves a red flag at us, to turn
away and do something different. If we become more
aware of our trauma responses due to a perceived threat
– like fight (being ready for the charge), flight (bolting),
freeze (becoming immobilized), flop (collapsing), and
fawn (pleasing) – we have a better chance to experience
freedom when we are triggered.

The intention here is to recognize the triggers, so we
can have some freedom. We will always experience
a trigger of some kind. I like to call this the elastic band
effect. Remember as a child when you would pull an
elastic band and feel the slight ping of sensations as
it snapped back? Some triggers feel like this. There's
the sting, and then the urge to act dissipates. This is
freedom. However, some triggers can feel like a tsunami
rushing through the body, and it can take time to
regulate the nervous system.

Some of the root causes of triggers

There are three main types of high-risk situations that contribute to triggers:

- negative mental states that are downers, or positive mental states that give rise to the thinking, *Let's celebrate, go out and party, buy a bottle of champagne, or have a blow out* when something good happens;
- interpersonal conflicts like a difference of opinion at work, or disagreements with our friends and family;
- and peer pressure to be part of the group, or pressure to join in with certain behaviors.

All of these situations can be triggers, putting us on the vicious cycle of conflict. These triggers impact us because we are often on automatic pilot. Often you hear someone in recovery say, "I don't understand how I picked up again." This happens because our behavior has become so automatic. Some of us may have had the experience of having an appointment at the end of the day. But when we jump into the car, or onto a motorbike, or cycle, or even begin walking at the end of our work day, where do we end up? Outside our front door – because we have been on automatic pilot and habitually done what we've always

15

done when we leave work at the end of the day. That is, to go home.

And this is similar to what can happen to us when we have been triggered. Without awareness, we pick up our choice of distraction. Because that is what we have always done. Without awareness, we can become verbally and/or physically abusive. Our mental states are often cluttered with many internal triggers. When emotions like anger, anxiety, depression, fear, loneliness, sadness, happiness, excitement occur, this can trigger us.

External triggers can become internal triggers. And internal triggers can become external triggers. For example, if we are in an argument with somebody, we can be experiencing some low-level irritation, and unconsciously we are wanting to move away from it. We could decide to take a walk to cool down, but on our walk we see people having a good time in the park, drinking cans of beer, smoking marijuana, and laughing. Without us being aware of it, the group of people have lifted our emotions a bit, we experience some lightness, and, before we know it, we have sought out the place where we could pick up our choice of distraction.

The important thing to remember is that anything can be a trigger. In fact, on some days, we see something and it has no impact on our mental states or actions, whereas, on another day, we experience the same stimulus and it has become a big trigger. We have hundreds of triggers.

We cannot avoid our triggers. Yes, it is good to become aware of them, because it can help us to be vigilant if we know we are going to be in an environment where these triggers may be present. However, we must be aware that, in any moment, we could be triggered. Sometimes sadness arises in us for no reason we can identify. Sometimes we are taken by surprise, and not prepared when somebody puts a drink in our hand, or serves us up food that we can't eat, or we are handed a magazine with images that trigger us, or we're invited out to a casino.

The trigger is the first arrow that has contact through one of the sense doors, and inevitably there is some kind of pain. For example, if our car is stolen, the first arrow of contact will be when we go to find our car, and our eyes notice it's not in its parking spot. There will be a physical sensation in the body, which will be unpleasant. This unpleasant pain intensifies because we stab ourselves with a second arrow that is often full of toxic interpretations, perceptions, and stories about who may have stolen it, and about the area it was parked in. This will cause a lot of suffering. They are well-worn stories that we have been playing over and over again. The trigger is such a small part of our pain, and yet our triggers can unleash a lot of suffering. It is possible to stay with the sensation of the first arrow. This can be very challenging for many, however, so we have to pay attention to that second dart of pain.

Patrick Carnes writes: "We create an independent inner observer that monitors and recognizes what's going on in our brain. This gives us the ability to step back and look at ourselves in much the same way that we look at others."[2]

RUST

Practice

ONE-MINUTE REFLECTION

When we are afflicted by the second arrow of suffering, we need to pull it out before our minds accumulate more rust. When you experience activation in the body, for example, like uncomfortable sensations of heat or tension, see if you can bring one of these reflections to mind:

R *Recognize you have been triggered*
U *Understand you are caught in a story*
S *Stretch, sing, stand, sway with sensations*
T *Tell the story to relax and trust that this shall pass*

This practice does not have to be linear: we can call on any of the letters for medicine when we are triggered. We can also practice RUST when we are calm, and cultivate some more freedom.

FIVE-MINUTE REFLECTION

Again, you can just focus on one of the letters for five minutes, or go through each letter in any order that works for you:

R Relax and recognize what is activating you right now. Pause and really see if you can catch what is whirling around your mind. Recognize that whatever is activating you is full of subjective perceptions and judgments.

U Understand that you are caught up in a story. A very old story. A story full of judgments, perceptions, resentments. A story that changes every time you replay it in your mind. Ask yourself, *What is the story? Why am I still holding on to the story? What is it doing for me? Is this story true?*

S Sit with the sensations in the body. Stand with sensations. Stretch with sensations. Sway the body with sensations. Sing with sensations or even silently scream with sensations. See if you can feel any tension or restriction in your body. What does it feel like? Where are the sensations located in the body? Place a hand where you feel these sensations and give this part of your body some kindness. Just know that the body is remembering past traumas, past hurts, past wounds.

Trust that this too shall pass. If we are still obsessing, or captured by the story, just ask the story to relax, to step aside for a moment so you can have some freedom.

Trust that these sensations are changing all the time. You won't always feel this pain or discomfort. If the story of what happened is still playing in your head, tell it to be quiet. Ask it to relax, so you can let go of all the rust that has accumulated in your life… So you can be at peace. Know that "this too shall pass" is an old mindfulness teaching of impermanence. The Dalai Lama was once asked to describe the Buddhist teachings. His response was: "Everything changes." We all know this teaching is true – just look in a mirror, can you honestly say you look exactly the same as you did five years ago?

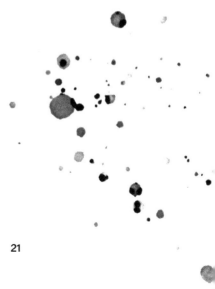

EXPLORING OUR TRIGGERS

A TWENTY-MINUTE REFLECTION

The good news is that we can prepare for those unexpected occasions when triggers seem to arise out of the blue.

First, begin to identify what some of your triggers are. Second, learn to take a deep breath when you wake up in the morning:

- take a deep breath before you leave the house;
- take a deep breath when you arrive at your destination;

- take a deep breath when you leave your destination and when you arrive back home.

One intentional deep simple breath five times a day can help to break the automatic pilot syndrome and slow down the process of the vicious cycle. There is nothing wrong with being activated – all of us have triggers that bring up feelings we find unpleasant, pleasant, or neutral. When we have been triggered, we have to learn to soothe our direct experience with breath, gentleness, and kindness. We can always use the excuse that we need the washroom, and we can privately take all the breaths we need before coming out to face our world again. We can take a breath at our work station, or in the driver's seat of a car before we put the keys in the ignition.

There are so many opportunities in the day to take one deep breath, and, if we remember just once to take a breath, it will have an impact.

I invite you to begin a list of all the things that can trigger you. And to keep the list open, because you may find yourself adding to it while reading this book. Try not to get into a long narrative. As best you can, be specific. For example, a trigger may be eating alone, or it could be seeing people having a good time, or images on the computer, or the way someone speaks to you, or a falling out with a friend or a sibling.

Each time you write down a trigger, allow yourself
to take a deep breath in. Then, as you breathe out,
expand the breath throughout your whole body.
And just become aware of what you are feeling
or experiencing in that moment. As best you can,
turn toward the feeling with kindness and without
judgment.

LIST OF
TRIGGERS

~

- _____
  _____
- _____
  _____
- _____
  _____
- _____
  _____
- _____
  _____

3

COMING
HOME
TO THE BODY

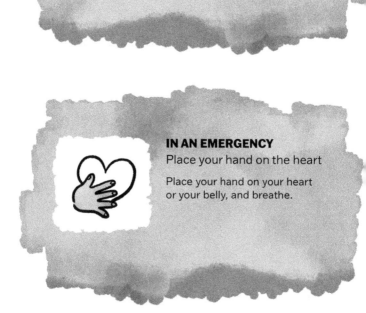

INSIDE THE KIT
Inhaler

The Breath.
Remember to breathe.

IN AN EMERGENCY
Place your hand on the heart

Place your hand on your heart
or your belly, and breathe.

TIP

Go for a walk and feel the earth beneath
your feet, the moisture in the air, the wind
on your face, and the heat in your body
as you move. Know with every step the
earth feels us, and we too can feel the earth
if we breathe. This is how we come home
to the body. Ask yourself, *When did I stop
breathing deeply?*

Freedom within the body

Mindfulness teaches us to come back to the body.
The journey of freedom is learning to find our way back
to the body that is our home. Many of us have become
identified with the cell phone, the iPad, the laptop,
often scrolling for hours, and losing ourselves in
mindless information. And some of us have lost our
way home, because our bodies were violated in
childhood and/or adulthood. We have to relearn that
our body can be one of the safest places we could ever
inhabit. The breath is the guide back into the body.
In the last chapter, we explored triggers and how to work
with them. In this chapter, we will look at the impact
of triggers on the body.

Many of us have lost our way home to the body. We
switched all feelings off. All the sense doors closed.
To protect ourselves, we made sure nobody was at home
in our body. If we are able to find our way home and
turn all the feelings back on in the body, we will have
some more freedom.

Some of us have left our bodies because of debilitating
pain, or due to struggling with a disability. And
there are those of us who find the process of aging so
challenging that we have left our bodies too. Some

of us can have complex relationships to our bodies, thinking they're not beautiful enough, or the right shape, size, or skin color. Leaving the body has also been a trauma response for those of us who have been physically or sexually abused and/or raped. There are so many reasons why we leave our bodies, and so many reasons why we find it difficult to come home to the body. The body also houses many uncomfortable sensations that are implicit memories that cannot yet be verbalized, and in turn can fracture the mind/heart.

Coming home to the body can also be difficult because many of us who have had addictions have spent a lifetime splitting from the body: getting out of our heads, chasing altered states, wanting to be high or numb. In mindfulness, we are saying: come back to the body, come back to the breathing, inhabit your body, and be in direct experience with whatever is arising in the now.

The body is the home for all of us. It's where we live all our lives, and, if we are not at peace in our body, we will not be at peace in any other areas of our lives. We have to learn to befriend our body, and not treat it like an enemy. And know it is safe to have our feelings now. The body can become our best friend. Sensations in the body will warn us when we are at risk.

Learn to play in the body

Let's play a little. Imagine your body as the perfect car, or motorcycle, or push-bike. All these vehicles have brakes, and we use the brakes to stop us from having an accident. Imagine you are driving your body around, and every time you are triggered it becomes a red traffic light. Use the breath to apply the brakes, to help pause the body. The breath is with us all the time, and we can use it to put the brakes on the trigger, which in turn will stop us acting out or picking up our choice of substance, distraction, or compulsive behavior. It will also help to interrupt the often unhelpful flow of compulsive thinking.

The breath is the way back to our body. When we allow ourselves to breathe fully and experience the touch of the breathing, we will find our way back home to the body. Coming home to the body means coming home to breathing. We can learn to soothe the body and mind/heart by connecting to the touch of the breathing.

Our body is our home, and we have to learn to comfort it. When we can comfort the body, we can begin to learn to be comfortable in our body, and then we can be comfortable anywhere. When we are back in touch with

COMING HOME TO THE BODY

the body, it will become our best friend, a lover, a parent. It will take care of us. We will begin to experience sensations in the body that we have ignored. These sensations will no longer be triggers for us to turn away from: they will be warning signs to remind us we need to come home to the body.

I learned at the age of fourteen that home was in the body. I was moving for the umpteenth time, and was trying to pack a record player into my suitcase. I remember feeling such pangs of sadness in my throat. I sat down, cried, and then realized the only thing I had been taking with me every time I moved was my body. I understood right then that home was in my body. With nobody to share this insight with, I spent the next twenty years in protest, not wanting to feel such pain in the body, and not wanting to be in touch with the breath. I was completely uncomfortable in my body, and this was expressed through disordered eating. I couldn't even look at my body's reflection in a mirror or a shop window.

I was unable to connect to the breath. It seemed so daunting, and I know I am not alone. Many people find it traumatic to begin connecting to the breath. For example, the desperate cry "I can't breathe" has come to represent the oppression experienced by the black and Hispanic communities in the USA, as they face the brutality of law enforcement. Similarly, it points to the detrimental impact of war. It is only by ensuring our safety that we can exercise our inherent right to breathe.

Through the practice of dancing, I unconsciously learned to come home to the body. Sounds and movement guided me home. For me it was most traumatic coming home to taste and smells. And finally I was able to surrender to the breath. For you, it may be traumatic coming home to the body too, and so our doorway to coming fully home to the body is through one of the sense doors of touch, sound, taste, smell, sight, and the mind.

No separation

Remember our body is not separate from earth. It is solid like earth. We eat from the earth, we give back to the earth. We cannot live without earth. Remember our body is not separate from water. We drink fluids and our body is full of fluids. We cannot live without water. Remember our body is not separate from fire. We need heat, our body is heat, we cannot live without fire. Remember our body is not separate from the wind.

We breathe in and out, our body belches and farts, we cannot live without wind.

The body is with us 24/7: wherever we go, the body comes with us.

The founder of mindfulness, Buddha Shakyamuni, teaches us to breathe through all experience. And, in the first foundation of mindfulness, he teaches that we should focus on the body. Learning to experience breathing in the body.[3]

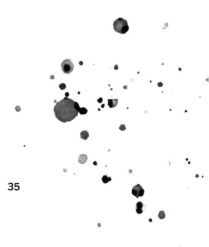

A PRACTICE OF LOVE

ONE-MINUTE REFLECTION

When we are split from the body and find it difficult to be in the body, we need to cultivate some self-love. When you are aware of disassociating or leaving your body, see if you can call just one of these to mind:

L *Love and/or like an aspect of yourself*
O *Own your uniqueness*
V *Validate your existence*
E *Enjoy your body*

FIVE-MINUTE REFLECTION

Again, you can just spend five minutes on one of these reflections in any order that works for you. Or go through the whole new meaning of LOVE:

L Loving or liking every bit of yourself, regardless of your skin color, race, religion, gender, or abilities. Find something you love about your body – feet, or hands, or the way you stand, or the shape of your elbows, or your smile, your eyes, your hair.

Allow the word "love" to reverberate in your body. Hear yourself say, *I love my skin color, I love my race, I love who I am*. How does it feel in your body to hear yourself say this? Breathe into your whole body, relax, and ask any criticizing voice to relax so you can feel some love today.

O Owning your uniqueness, opening up to your authentic self. What is it that you like about your skin color, your race, gender, sexuality? As you reflect on this question, become aware of any tension in the body and relax.

V Validating your existence. Do not let anybody ever tell you again that you are less than anybody else. Stop believing that something is wrong with you, that you don't have the right to be here. Feel the fullness of your presence. Place a hand upon your body and feel the warmth of your own hand validating you.

E Eliminating all the slurs that have been projected onto you. Touch into the sadness caused by some of the harmful things that have been said to you. Allow yourself to feel the tears, wet tears or dry tears.

Now put all the slurs you've ever experienced into an imaginary paper bag or wooden box, and visualize yourself burning it on a fire. Just watch it burning up and disappearing.

And now say the word "love" again, this time with a new meaning – *I love every bit of myself, I own my uniqueness, I validate my presence, I extinguish all the prejudicial baggage I have been carrying around* – and let it go.

TWENTY-MINUTE REFLECTION

Learning to breathe again through the ancient method of the mindfulness of breathing, just focusing on the first tetrad.[4]

- Become aware of the breath without changing the way you breathe. Just simply notice the length of the breath: notice if it is a long breath, short breath, in-between breath – or even a "don't know" breath. It doesn't matter how long the in-breath or the out-breath is, just become familiar and friends with your breath.

- Become aware of the quality of your breathing. Simply notice if it is a calm breath, an agitated breath, a neutral breath, an excited breath, a sleepy breath. Your thoughts or thinking will give you a clue as to the quality of your breathing. The breath may be smooth, rough, anxious, joyful. It doesn't matter what the breath feels like. What is important is for you to become familiar with your breathing. Become friends with your breath.
- Now become sensitive to the body, sensitive to your breathing, and begin experiencing your whole body breathing – experiencing the breathing from head to toe.
- Become aware of the touch of the breath upon the body. If you are new to meditation, just become aware of the touch of the breath upon the abdomen, rising and falling. If you have a regular practice, become aware of the touch of the breath on the upper lip and inside the nostril. It will be cool when you breathe in and warmer when you breathe out. Notice the sensations as you experience the touch of the breath: this can be itchy, tickling, warm, pulsating. And even if you say to yourself *I feel nothing*, know there is always feeling, and you may just want to touch the body to remind yourself of feeling.
- Now allow yourself to have a taste of freedom. Being one with the breathing and enjoying this precious moment in the here and now. Nothing to do, just let the body breathe you.

"

Heart like an ocean:
just as the waves in an ocean arise and cease,
allow your feelings and emotions to arise and cease.

4

TO FEEL
OR NOT
TO FEEL?

INSIDE THE KIT
First aid manual

There are only three kinds of feelings: pleasant, unpleasant, neutral. If you want an extra feeling in the kit, then have a mixture of all these three.

IN AN EMERGENCY
Stretching

Stretch the body, and notice the body as you stretch.

TIP

When you are feeling angry, abandoned,
unloved, unseen, know that this is not a
feeling – it is a story, an interpretation
of your experience. What we often think
of as feelings are actual perceptions.
Feeling is hedonic tone in the body that
is either pleasant, unpleasant, or neutral.
And each of these feelings can be a trigger.

Feeling tone

The founder of mindfulness, Buddha Shakyamuni, taught us that there are three hedonic feelings: unpleasant, pleasant, and neutral. Neutral is that place where we may experience boredom, so we want to spice our life up a bit, have something big happening in our lives. And so neutral swiftly changes to unpleasant or pleasant. When we are bored, we can pick a fight or start an argument to help us feel alive, or to be noticed. If we grew up in a household where there was much chaos, neutral can become a very unsafe feeling tone in the body, because we are waiting for the next drama to arise, and hence neutral becomes unpleasant.

Buddha Shakyamuni also taught the *Honeyball Sutta*,[5] where he explains that experience starts with contact – and that contact is with an external object or internal stimulus with one of the six senses (the sixth sense is the mind). When there is contact with one or more of the sense doors, this will give rise to one of the feeling tones in the body.

When one or more of the six senses encounters an external stimulus – like seeing colors, or smelling baked goods, or hearing a scream, or touching a sharp edge, or tasting something bitter, or an internal stimulus like a thought or emotion – there is contact. And based on the initial contact there will be a feeling tone in the body that is unpleasant, pleasant, or neutral (nothing much going on).

The body may experience butterflies in the stomach, or an itchy groin. We may even salivate, or feel tension in our jaw. Whatever we experience will be an early warning sign when we are at risk. We may need to remove ourselves from the current situation. Instead of pushing these subtle sensations away, we turn toward them and say, *Oh, I'm at risk, I'm experiencing vulnerability right now, I need to walk away, sit down and take a breath.*

When we accept these sensations and embrace them, it allows for the space where we can make wiser decisions.

Feeling tone is very different from what we often call feeling. Feeling tone is sensation in the body that can be experienced as pleasant, unpleasant, or neutral. Sometimes feeling tone is described as hedonic tone, sensations in the body. Understanding that sensations in the body only fall into three feelings of pleasant, unpleasant, and neutral can help us become aware that sensations act as an alarm bell warning us we are feeling vulnerable, or there may be a threat to our safety, or we are happy and excited. Feeling tone is different from emotions, and we will explore this later in the book.

Take a moment, and become aware of the sensations in your body right now, and then ask yourself, *Are they pleasant, unpleasant, or neutral?* If you are holding this book in your hand, does that feel smooth, rough, cold? If you listening to the book right now, what does the voice feel like to your ears – harsh, scratchy, echoey? Where are your feet right now? What do your feet feel like inside a shoe, or in a sock or stocking, or on a carpet or floor? Do your feet feel cold, tense, relaxed, hot, buzzy?

Feeling tone is sometimes referred to as our internal barometer. Just as a barometer can tell us about the weather, our internal barometer can help us to read our internal weather. It can act as an early warning system, to let us know when things are starting to get difficult and to warn us that we need to pay attention to what is happening. Remember excitement and happiness can be triggers – these emotions are activation in the body.

Learning to connect to feeling tone is imperative: this awareness can make the difference between preventing and spiralling into another round of bad habits and relapse.

Staying with feeling tone in the body is often painful, partly because many of us have suppressed feelings and sensations with the help of stimulants and compulsive behaviors. Many of us only know the highs and the lows, and nothing in between. We're not interested in the neutral feeling tone or emotions because we want the big experience, the big aha moment, the big high. And the subtlety of sadness, hurt, pain, pleasure, joy can be excruciating for some people to stay with.

Pema Chödrön, the celebrated Buddhist nun, says: "Lean into the sharp points and fully experience all of them." [6] And these sharp points are in the feeling tone, not in all the thoughts that we can have while trying to avoid our direct experience of the body. We think that if we allow ourselves to experience feeling tone, this will trigger us to pick up our choice of distraction. But often we are triggered because our mind has been captured by so many thoughts that mindless obsessing about our behaviors arises.

How we interpret external or internal events will also impact how we feel. Therefore, it's important for us to learn about our internal barometer.

Bringing mindfulness to pleasant events can be a way of experiencing without adding any extra thoughts, such as craving for something, or wishing the pleasant experience will last forever.

It can also help us to notice subtle positive things arising in our experience, which we tend not to notice if we have a hangover, a come down, or are feeling depressed after a binge with one of our compulsive behaviors.

When we bring mindfulness to unpleasant feeling tone in the body, it will alert us to triggers we didn't know we had. It can also help us to notice subtle negative thoughts arising in our experience, which can undermine our recovery without us being conscious of it.

Some of us find it incredibly difficult to be with pleasant hedonic tone in the body. If we were sexually assaulted as a child, we can sometimes become disgusted with pleasant sensations, because we know that when the body is touched in a particular way, it produces feeling tone that we have no control over. Some of us may have experienced a pleasant sensation amidst all other sensations, and pleasant becomes nasty, dangerous, scary.

Some of us have become so attached to feeling unpleasant because of our childhood conditioning that we find it scary to let go. All feeling tones are activating, and we have to learn to be calm, and trust they too shall pass.

Understanding feelings

Mindfulness teaches us that the body will produce feeling, and that feeling tone in the body is unavoidable. We cannot escape feeling. But what we can do is begin to notice that the feeling tone is a sensation in the body – pleasant, unpleasant, or neutral. And, given space, it will change and even dissipate. That's what the body does: it produces a feeling tone that is either pleasant, unpleasant, or neutral.

Viveka Chen, a dear friend, Buddhist teacher, and somatic social justice facilitator, has created a list to help us understand feeling tone. She introduces four categories to help us name our sensations. And of course all of these will then fall into the category of pleasant, unpleasant, or neutral, and sometimes a mixture of all three:

1. **Temperature:** warm, cool, icy, cold, hot

2. **Density:** soft, hard, tight, empty, expanding, compacting
3. **Energy:** itchy, tingling, goosebumpy, trembling, radiating, pounding, still, streaming, flowing, pulsing
4. **Numbness:** numb, fuzzy, faint, frozen

Once upon a time, I could never experience sadness in the body. The feeling tone of sadness in my body was like somebody wringing a towel dry in my throat, and no tears would splash from my eyes – there were just the intense unpleasant sensations in my throat.

I had so much aversion for this unpleasant feeling in my body that I swiftly pushed it away. I was afraid that I would be overwhelmed by this pain in the body. I avoided going to the cinema because this was the one place where I occasionally would lose control over my bodily functions and a few tears would roll down my cheek. I took pride in being able to make myself happy. I was a master at making myself happy, or so I thought.

My way of making myself happy would be to go out partying all night, snort a line, drop a pill, and drink champagne. And when I was coming down two days later, I moved away from the groggy unpleasant feelings in my body and went on a binge and purged. I was on a vicious cycle of the enslavement of my mind.

When I began meditating thirty-three years ago, I was gobsmacked at how often the feeling tone in the body changed. I was also surprised at the range of emotions I could have in one hour. Sadness, joy, anger, irritation all came flooding in when I was able to begin sitting with unpleasant, pleasant, and neutral feeling tone, without turning away from the experience in the body.

We may want to relieve the discomfort quickly. This can lead to craving for familiar, habitual behavior, coupled with thoughts that facilitate the relapse process, like *With all this struggle, I deserve a drink*. In this vulnerable state, if we then find ourselves in a high-risk situation like an argument (which we may semi-consciously have engineered), it may be very difficult not to return to addictive behavior.

The feeling tone, thoughts, judgments, and emotions can all reinforce each other, as we work ourselves up into a more and more negative state.

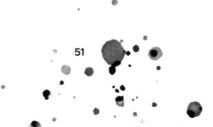

51

WORKING WITH FEAR

ONE-MINUTE REFLECTION

Often we are fearful of feeling sensations in the body, of experiencing feeling in the body. When fear arises in the mind, call to mind this reflection:

FEAR simply stands for False Evidence Appearing Real.

Reflect on a story you have been recycling over the years and ask yourself, *Is it really true? Is it actually happening now?* Know that stories from the past are happening only in your head and nowhere else. As you replay the story, become aware of the sensations in your body: are they pleasant, unpleasant, or neutral?

FIVE-MINUTE REFLECTION

Face Everything And Relax. Know that feeling tone is always changing, and, if we are able to relax, sensations won't become so overwhelming. So allow yourself five minutes to turn toward whatever is happening in the body, and just surrender and relax.

TWENTY-MINUTE REFLECTION

First become aware of feeling tone. You become aware of feeling tone by noticing sensations in the body.

So let's do a body scan together. (If you have a history of sexual and/or physical trauma, I suggest you do this practice with a mentor, a friend, or someone who can hold you if you are activated. Meanwhile, just place a hand on a part of your body you are comfortable with and breathe.)

Notice your left foot: is it feeling pleasant, unpleasant, or neutral?

Notice your right foot: is it feeling pleasant, unpleasant, or neutral?

Notice your left leg: is it feeling pleasant, unpleasant, or neutral?

Notice your right leg: is it feeling pleasant, unpleasant, or neutral?

Notice your torso: is it feeling pleasant, unpleasant, or neutral?

Notice your left arm: is it feeling pleasant, unpleasant, or neutral?

Notice your right arm: is it feeling pleasant, unpleasant, or neutral?

Notice your left shoulder: is it feeling pleasant, unpleasant, or neutral?

Notice your right shoulder: is it feeling pleasant, unpleasant, or neutral?

Notice your neck: is it feeling pleasant, unpleasant, or neutral?

Notice your head: is it feeling pleasant, unpleasant, or neutral?

Notice what you are feeling right now and write it down.

Notice that there can be several different feeling tones experienced in the body at the same time, and yet our mind can be captured just by one feeling tone. Learning to expand the awareness throughout our whole body can help us calm the nervous system, and cultivate equanimity if we find ourselves triggered by an event.

I AM
FEELING...

~

- _____
  _____
- _____
  _____
- _____
  _____
- _____
  _____
- _____
  _____

"

Thoughts are like clouds: just as you get dark clouds
and bright clouds that come and go, know that
your thoughts will also be sometimes dark and sometimes
bright, and let them too come and go.

5

IT'S
JUST
A
THOUGHT

INSIDE THE KIT
Muscle relaxant

Thoughts are not facts – relax your thoughts.

IN AN EMERGENCY
Stop

Stop believing your thoughts.

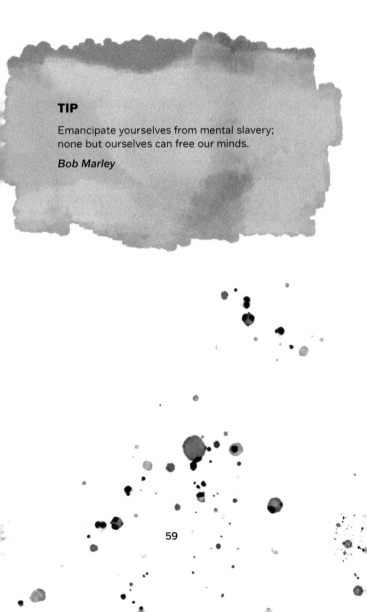

TIP

Emancipate yourselves from mental slavery;
none but ourselves can free our minds.

Bob Marley

Thoughts are often not the truth

When we are controlled by our thoughts, we make interpretations, believing our thoughts to be true. Based on those interpretations, we make decisions, which can impact our lives. Thoughts are just mental events arising and passing, like all other events in our lives. They are often task orientated, like *I must finish cleaning the house*, or self-reflective, like *I could have dealt with things differently*, or concerned with past or future events, like *I can't wait to go on holiday*. These mental events then shape our emotions, perceptions, and inner dialogue – our entire life.

I used to think we were totally powerless over our thoughts. That thoughts were inevitable because thinking is what the mind loves to do. Today, I can see clearly that, while much of our thinking is optional, some of our thoughts are optional too. What I do in this moment has an impact on the thoughts that arise in the next moment. For example, if I steal something in this moment, in the next moment my thoughts will be impacted. I will be worrying about whether anybody saw me, or about getting caught. Our actions influence our thoughts.

Types of thoughts

There are two broad categories of unhelpful thoughts: negative thoughts and facilitative thoughts. Negative thoughts are those that make a negative interpretation about the world, ourselves, or other people. How we interpret the world will affect how we feel. If we habitually fall into negative thinking, we are more likely to suffer.[7]

Negative thoughts are full of self-blame and/or shame: *I could have done that better, how stupid of me, the world is a horrible place, people are not safe.*

Facilitative thoughts are like rationalizations that can lead to abusive behaviors. For example, I have had a bad day at work, so I am justified in being angry when I return home. These rationalizations can also put people back on a vicious cycle of conflict and/or addiction.

Other types of negative thoughts can include the following, and all of us to some degree will recognize parts of our minds in this list:

• Intrusive thoughts are thoughts that are unwanted and involuntary. They can be distressing and sometimes disturbing. They can have an obsessive and repetitive quality to them.

- Judgmental thoughts are about evaluating, comparing, and forming opinions about people and ourselves, which are often incorrect.
- Obsessive thoughts capture the mind, control the mind, and dominate our thinking. They often focus on a specific theme, like a person, a thing, and/or fears.
- Delusional thoughts aren't based in reality and can arise out of false beliefs and/or mind altering substances.
- Anxious thoughts are dominated by worry and anxiety about things that may never happen and about future events, usually with negative outcomes.
- Prejudiced thoughts are grounded in hatred toward another group of people, race, religion, ethnicity, gender, sexuality. They can become so out of control that people can become racist, misogynistic, homophobic, and delusional.

Of course we can also have positive thoughts, which can be supportive of our mental states, and can sometimes have us living in a dream world:

- Rational thoughts involve critical thinking, and are often analytical and logical. These thoughts can help us problem-solve.

- Inspiring thoughts are creative, and inspire creative and artistic expression. They open up the imagination and give the possibility of optimism and happiness.
- Reflective thoughts help us to be more mindful and self-aware. They are introspective and explore our emotions and actions.
- Spontaneous thoughts are influenced by what we read, what we listen to. They are influenced by our gender, culture, sexuality, disabilities.
- Loving thoughts are kind-hearted, unbiased, receptive, impartial, neutral, unconditional.

Thoughts that dominate us and control us are often full of interpretations – so much so that we think all our thoughts are true. These thoughts impact our decisions to the extent that we make choices that can have a devastating effect on our mental and emotional health. We are unable to see the facts of a situation, and because of this we continue to loop around the cycle. Mindfulness teaches us to understand that a thought is just a mental occurrence, and it isn't necessarily a representation of reality. Thoughts are not necessarily facts. When we can begin to recognize this, it may lead to more helpful decisions and outcomes.

ONE-MINUTE REFLECTION

STOP – take time out from listening to your thoughts, and bring to mind one of these reflections:

S *Stop what you are doing*
T *Test your thought: is it true, is it helpful, is it harmful?*
O *Observe your thought*
P *Pause, and let your thought arise like a bubble and burst*

FIVE-MINUTE REFLECTION

Again, you can just spend five minutes on one of these reflections in any order that works for you. Or go through the whole new meaning of STOP:

S Stop identifying with your thoughts. Stop solidifying your thoughts. Stop becoming your thoughts. You are more than your thoughts.

T Trust that your thoughts will arise and cease if you don't begin thinking your thoughts and weaving a story.

O Observe your thoughts, become aware of the thoughts that trend in your mind, and get curious.

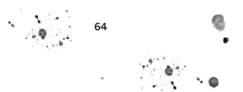

P Pause, stretch, rock or sway the body, gently interrupting your mind by bouncing up and down so you can drop into your body.

 **TWENTY-MINUTE REFLECTION**

We can begin to see that our thoughts are not facts – they are just mental events arising and passing, like all other events in our lives. We can easily take the thoughts that appear in our minds for granted. We assume that they are true, and believe that we must act on them. With mindfulness, we are trying to relate to our thoughts differently – not taking them so seriously or buying into the stories they are telling us.

When you react, remind yourself that you most probably identify with the story coursing through your mind and not the actual facts. It can be helpful to ask yourself, *What are the facts?* And sometimes we will realize we don't even know the facts, and that our behaviors are based on all our perceptions and interpretations. Ask yourself, *What assumptions am I making? What do I know to be really true?*

There are thoughts that I call **life sentences** that often have no factual truth to them.

Often I hear people say they are unlovable. I ask them: "Are you in a relationship, do you have good friends?," and they say: "Yes." I respond by saying: "How can you possibly be unlovable when you are in a romantic relationship and you have good friends? If you got this far in life, somebody must have loved you."

So let's begin to declutter the mind of some of these life sentences that have shaped our world and kept us trapped in a story.

I'm going to list some thoughts that tend to occur frequently in the mind:

- I'm unlovable…
- Nobody loves me…
- I'm a loser…
- I hate myself…
- I'm gross…

Write down some of your own life sentences, and ask yourself, *Whose voice is that in my head? Who or what shaped that voice in my head?* Try to see that these life sentences are things you were made to think about yourself in childhood.

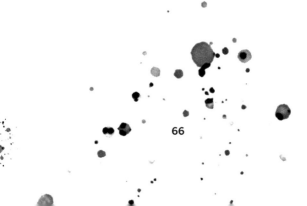

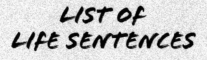

LIST OF
LIFE SENTENCES

~

- _____
  _____
- _____
  _____
- _____
  _____
- _____
  _____
- _____
  _____

If I said to you, "You have carrots growing out of your ears," would you believe it? No – so why do we believe some of these thoughts?

We need to remember that, while our thoughts can appear true, and we think they require acting on, we need to pause, because our thoughts are just thoughts and not absolute truths.

Ask yourself, *Are these thoughts really true?*

And, if you say yes, *How do you know they are true?*

And even if you can find evidence for the validity of the thoughts, ask yourself, *What other thought could I have that would change this thought I think of as true?*

The mind will produce thoughts. This is what the mind does. When we experience feeling tone, thoughts pop up, thoughts that try to protect us by taking us away from the experience in the body.

Now begin to resource yourself, and write down some positive, nourishing life sentences that will give you some emotional freedom:

- I am good at what I do…
- There are people who love me…
- I am courageous…

You choose your own.

LIST OF NOURISHING LIFE SENTENCES

~

- _____
  _____
- _____
  _____
- _____
  _____
- _____
  _____
- _____
  _____

6

EXCAVATING EMOTIONS

INSIDE THE KIT
Pain killer

Lift your head up, turn it side to side. Look up at the sky.

IN AN EMERGENCY
Buddha

Think to yourself or say out loud, *This is not me, this is not mine, this is not I.*

The Buddha

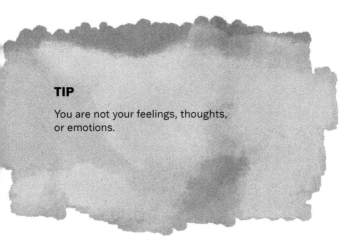

TIP

You are not your feelings, thoughts, or emotions.

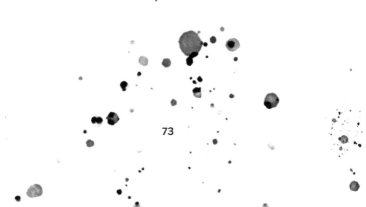

Emotions

Our thoughts and emotions shape our speech and bodily actions. In this chapter, I am inviting you to be with your emotions, like anger, while breathing into the body, and allowing your emotions to arise and cease like the waves in an ocean.

I used to be addicted to the emotions of excitement and amusement. I would do anything to feel high. I took pride in not ever feeling sad, or unhappy. Of course my emotions would swing from anger to excitement, and I never seemed to feel anything in between.

The first contact of pain was my trigger to make myself feel high. "When something traumatic happened in my life I would go out dancing all night, even without intoxicants."[8] The dancing made me feel momentarily better.

I was not aware that I was still suffering. I had many coping strategies to deal with all my pain. I would never have admitted to being depressed. But, when I look back on my life, I can see how I was self-medicating against the uncomfortable emotions of fear, sadness, and even disgust.

There are many theories around emotions. I like what Robert Plutchik suggests in his wheel of emotions. He says there are eight primary emotional dimensions: happiness vs. sadness, anger vs. fear, trust vs. disgust, and surprise vs. anticipation.[9]

These emotions can then be combined in a variety of ways. For example, happiness and anticipation might combine to create excitement.

Plutchik also says that these emotions are impacted by our particular experience, which includes our environment, poverty, living in a war zone, race, gender, sexuality, different abilities. So, while emotions are universal, they are impacted by our circumstances, and many of our thoughts about our circumstances will help to create emotions.

Emotions are also impacted by our physiological responses to things like chronic physical or mental pain. When our heart races, we can move into emotions like love or anger. When our eyes or nose or tongue has contact with our choice of substance, we can salivate, and this can produce emotions of excitement or fear.

Sometimes our emotions are in response to another person's behavior. For example, we may see someone's face frown, and our thoughts say, *Oh they don't like me*, and a passing emotion of irritation, sadness, or anger arises. Somebody we like smiles at us, a pleasant sensation arises in the body, our thoughts begin to tell us they like us, and the emotion of happiness or lust can arise.

Thoughts stir our emotions. And once we are in our emotions or moods, emotions that linger, we can begin to habitually push them away or force them down with our choice of substance or compulsive behaviors.

The problem is that pushing away painful thoughts and emotions usually makes them stronger if we never allow ourselves to face the pain. It's like trying not to think of a pink elephant – the more we try not to think of one, the more pink elephants show up in our minds.[10]

When we resist our thoughts, they persist. Suffering can come from our personal response to the mental or physical pain we experience. Therefore suffering is often our proliferation of thoughts that can turn into emotions like resentment, anger, hatred, or jealousy.

What if there was nobody to think our thoughts? I am not asking you to get rid of your thoughts, because the mind produces thoughts – it's what the mind loves to do. I'm inviting you to have thoughts without a thinker. Inviting you to get curious about your thoughts. And notice how they shape your emotions.

It's inevitable that you may want to say, *No more thoughts – I'm done with my thoughts that produce emotions like anger, jealousy, fear, and anxieties.* This is a normal response to thoughts and thinking that creates so much pain and suffering. However, pushing them away intensifies them, and they will continue to pop up.

Of course taking time out from our thinking and our emotions can be helpful. A child who is struggling at school can ask the teacher to take time out; the child knows time out is temporary, and will join the class again when they feel calmer. Similarly, we can take time out by distracting ourselves, and know that we do have to come back to the emotions that are disturbing us.

Mindfulness is inviting us to be with an emotion like anger, and begin to experience what anger is like in the body. When we can connect to anger in the body, we will be able to determine if it is unpleasant, pleasant, or neutral.

When things are pleasant, we tend to want more. For example, we may be out for dinner, enjoying the cuisine, and the contact of the food on our tongue and our nose will produce pleasant feeling tone in the body. Before we have finished the food on the plate, we are thinking, *When can I eat this again? I hope there is more.* The emotion of craving arises. The same process will happen with alcohol, drugs, gambling, gaming, surfing the internet, sex, love, and any other distractions we may indulge in.

When our experience is unpleasant, we tend to want to push it away. For example, it may be that we see a person who reminds us of someone who hurt us. The contact of this person upon our eyes will produce an unpleasant feeling tone in the body. Before we realize it, we have begun to spin a story about this person, telling ourselves we don't like them. The emotion of aversion arises and we may be unfriendly to this person, or a memory of the actual person who hurt us floods our mind, and we turn to an unhelpful habit to soothe ourselves.

We can end up playing a game of sensations that keeps us on the vicious cycle of shame. When something is pleasant, we move toward it because we want more;

when something is unpleasant, we move away from our immediate experience because we want less of the discomfort – we are never fully satisfied.

When emotions are neutral, we can become restless, even anxious, because nothing much is happening in our experience. I used to deliberately get trashed, because I believed I could cope much better when my life was in chaos. I didn't realize I told myself this story because, as a child, I had lived with a lot of big emotions like fear, disgust, hatred, anger, and I was scared of nothing much happening in my life.

The binge–vomit–intoxicant cycle created the drama I had learned to grow up with throughout my childhood and adolescence. I had to learn to honor my more neutral emotions, and thank the dramas I created in my life from my eating disorder for helping me move away from the scary neutral spaces. Instead of running away from them by taking intoxicants, I had to learn it was safe to be with nothing much happening in life.

Emotions on the vicious cycle are so important to understand, because this is one of the places where we can get caught in the relapse of unhelpful habits and behaviors.

ONE-MINUTE REFLECTION

SHAME is the emotion that accompanies the story that something is intrisically wrong with us. Let's bring to mind shame, an emotion that assails many of us, and redefine its meaning so it can support our healing. We can practice this even if we have behaved inappropriately. The past has gone, and we can not change our past actions with shame. We can learn to relate to the past with compassion and forgiveness.

Now bring to mind one of these reflections:

S *Stop blaming yourself – nothing is wrong with you*
H *Have the courage that you did your best*
A *Ask yourself, What do I need right now?*
M *Make a safe space for your wounded inner child*
E *Elevate yourself from survivor to someone living life to its fullest potential*

FIVE-MINUTE REFLECTION

Again, you can just spend five minutes on one of these reflections in any order that works for you. Or go through the whole new meaning of SHAME:

S Stop blaming yourself. Stop thinking, *I am bad*. Stop thinking, *Something is wrong with me*. Instead, get curious about what happened to you, that you ended up blaming yourself for something that you had no control over.

H Have confidence that you did your best. Can you accept you did your best right now? Know that these thoughts of *I'm bad*, *something is wrong with me* were most probably shaped by your childhood, and are an old story that has never been true. When you get caught in this loop of thought, know that the question is, *What happens to you when you have an attack of shame?*

A Ask yourself, *What do I really need?* When we are flooded with shame, old traumas have come to the surface. Old stories and perceptions come to haunt us. We are deregulated and we need to be held, to be heard, to be loved. Ask yourself, *What is it I need when flooded with shame?*

M Make a safe place for your wounded inner child. Making a safe space for our inner child allows us to use our imagination to support us when navigating difficult emotions. This safe place could be up in the sky, in the trees, by the beach, somewhere in your home, anywhere your imagination wants to take you. The only condition is that it has to be safe for you. Make this safe space, and let your inner child know you will always be there for them, and they can always go to this place to feel safe.

E Elevate yourself. When we move from victim mode to survivor mode, we can get stuck. There is more than surviving our traumatic and/or dysfunctional pasts. We can begin living a life that is free of the past.

We need to extinguish all the painful things done to us in the past. We can choose how to extinguish some of these things. And sometimes we have to do this several times, until the memories stop sabotaging our happiness. We can release painful memories into a big fire – so imagine building it, and throwing on it all the fuel that has kept you consumed with shame. Keep on throwing it onto the fire, even after this practice has finished. Or you may want the wind to sweep these memories away with one full gust. You choose what you think is the best way to extinguish this toxic fuel that never ever belonged to you.

Sometimes we have to admit that perhaps we did something that was harmful. Rather than beating ourselves up with shame, we need to acknowledge the conditions that led to something, and then take responsibility for the harm we have caused. Be gentle with yourself by acknowledging you perhaps acted out of hurt and fear or low self-esteem.

TWENTY-MINUTE REFLECTION

What are some of the factors that can impact my emotions?

- my stinking thinking
- when I have chronic physical or mental pain
- my environment
- my gender, race, sexuality, disability

In this reflection, we will focus on a teaching often attributed to the great Buddhist monk Dogen, who lived in Japan in the twelfth century: "Body like the mountain, heart like the ocean, and mind like the sky."

This teaching will help us move in the world upright and with dignity, and invite us to turn toward our emotions with calm. Just sit, stand, or lie wherever you are, and repeat one or more of these phrases. Which one speaks to you the most?

Body like a mountain.
Just as a mountain is strong, firm, present, allow your body to be strong, firm, present too.

Heart like an ocean.
Just as the waves in an ocean arise and cease, allow your feelings and emotions to arise and cease.

Mind like the sky.
Just as the sky is wide and open, allow your mind to be wide and open.

Breath like an anchor.
Just as an anchor steadies a boat, allow your breath to steady your body whenever an emotion arises.

"

Thinking like a river: just as a river is fluid,
flows, and holds on to nothing, allow your thinking
to be fluid, flow, and hold on to nothing whatsoever.

7

THOUGHTS WITHOUT A STINKER

INSIDE THE KIT
Tweezers

Pinch yourself – a pinch can interrupt the flow of thinking and bring you back in the now. Take hold of your thumb and squeeze it gently until you are relaxed and regulated again.

IN AN EMERGENCY
Move

Get up and move. Move around the house. Get out of the environment that has activated a whole slew of thinking.

TIP

Know that, when you are assailed by
an uncontrollable proliferation of thinking,
a young part of you is present in the now.
That part of you wants to be seen, listened
to, or believed.

Stinking thinking

It's said that we have thousands of thoughts each day, and many of them we are not even aware of, despite the fact they can shape our decisions and behaviors. Our thoughts will be impacted by the news, by the things we listen to and read, by our past conditioning. Sometimes these thoughts can be quite alarming, even distasteful, and unwanted. However, we often don't act on such thoughts. For example, we may be waiting for a train, and a random thought can arise: *Let's jump*. But you don't – you move back. Or you are driving a car, and a strange thought may arise: *I am invincible – I can put my foot down on the accelerator*. And most of the time you don't act on these thoughts, but they leave you thinking, *Where did that come from?*

Lack of sleep, stress, watching gory films can impact your thoughts. Some of our thoughts are negative, and some are positive and constructive. There are those repetitive thoughts that can induce that stinking thinking. Stinking thinking makes up the stories we tell ourselves. These stories are the superego disguised in the voice of a negative parent or adult, who told us unkind things in childhood. Stinking thinking is often Energy Gone Overboard or EGO.

Thirty years ago, I woke up in my bed startled, and blurted out, "Oh my God, my biggest addiction is my stinking thinking." I was shocked. I had thought that, to get healthy, all I had to do was let go of alcohol, recreational stimulants, cigarettes, caffeine, and purging.

But I could see why I had been masking my feelings and thinking, because it was so overwhelming when I became aware of what I was saying to myself. I had been beating myself up with phrases like: *I hate myself*, *nobody loves me*, *I'm a loser*, and many more negative thoughts. I had to learn to have thoughts without a stinker.

My stinking thinking has been a matter of life and death. I lived in the hell realm of my head, which beat me up every time a whiff of emotions like vulnerability or sadness arose. I would tell myself I hated myself, and then my mind would become captured by all the reasons why I should hate myself, and I found myself trapped in the prison of my head. I used to think the only way out of my head was by taking my life. I'm so glad I was not successful at age thirteen, fifteen, and eighteen. However, I'm aware that my compulsive behaviors almost killed me, and I'm lucky to be alive. I have learned from experience that our thoughts become less intrusive and more spacious if we learn to relax the mind.

What is your story of thoughts and thinking?

The founder of mindfulness, Buddha Shakyamuni, gave a teaching to help working with distracting thoughts. He realized that part of the human malady is the capacity to think, which can create unnecessary suffering in our lives. The *Vitakkasanthana Sutta* suggests five ways to remove distracting thoughts and to work with debilitating thoughts. In brief, the Buddha suggests we begin simply and, if all else fails, move on to the next suggestion. The five ways fall into these categories:

- replacing your thoughts;
- reflecting on the results of your thoughts;
- redirecting your thoughts;
- reviewing your thoughts by becoming curious about what gave rise to the thoughts;
- restraining your thoughts.

Any one of these can work, and there are some vivid images to help us work with the suggestions. It does not

have to be a linear practice. For example, the fifth way
suggests we should resist and restrain thoughts, if all
else fails – this was the one that helped shatter the belief
that nobody cares about me:

*As – with their teeth clenched and their tongue pressed
against the roof of their mouth – a person beats down,
constrains, and crushes their mind with their awareness,
those evil, unskillful thoughts are abandoned and
subside. With their abandoning, the person steadies
their mind right within, settles it, unifies it, and
concentrates it.*[11]

On my fiftieth birthday, I was leading a call-and-
response ritual at the Buddhist center when my
mind suddenly became consumed by thoughts about
someone who had not turned up for my birthday.
I was so overwhelmed by the story of "nobody cares
about me, I'm not important, not good enough" that,
for a nano-moment, I was unable to continue with
the ritual. And then from nowhere I screamed
silently to myself STOP! The silent "stop" was so
forceful that something shattered, I was able to
continue with the ritual, and I have not been assailed
with those stories again. I was able to relax and calm
my mind.

However, let's look at the other four ways to help tame the mind in more detail, to help free it from fabrication and illusions.

The Buddha advises that, if our mind becomes consumed with something like aversion, jealousy, desire, or greed, then we counter this thought with loving-kindness. He uses the image of a carpenter knocking out a coarse peg for a fine one. If we are able to introduce an alternative way of thinking, it's said this will help to get rid of unwanted thoughts.

The Buddha also advises, if the first way doesn't work, that we imagine ourselves wearing all our thinking and intrusive thoughts like a rotting carcass around our neck all day. Here we are being advised to reflect on the consequences of our thinking. By objectifying our thoughts, we can begin to see more clearly. This practice helped me throw the rotting carcass of racism to the kerb. I could see clearly how I had internalized so much racism that it had filled me with anger and hatred. Once I could see how rotten these thoughts were, I abandoned them, and began to see the true reflection of myself in the mirror. I was no longer what society had projected on to me – a black angry woman.

If this fails, the Buddha advises us not to identify with the thought, and to ignore the thinking when it arises. We are encouraged to distract ourselves.

The fourth way is to ponder on removing the thoughts. The Buddha uses the analogy of a person walking fast, who asks themselves, *Why I am walking so fast?* This inquiry allows the person to slow down, and reflect on why they are moving so fast. It's hoped that this would help the person to stop and just sit, or even lie down.

You might find that some of this traditional Buddhist advice feels unhelpfully harsh, aggressive, or disdainful when you try it out with your thoughts. Instead, you might want to try a more contemporary approach, for example, from the Internal Family Systems (IFS) modality. IFS teaches that our thoughts are just trying to protect us, and need to be responded to with love and self-comforting as a means of transformation.[12]

This is an invitation to experiment with one of these suggestions and see what happens.

The Buddha also taught that pain is inevitable, but suffering is optional. He taught that, if we try to move away from our pain, we will multiply the pain – it will become a thought, an emotion, and a story about the pain, which will create more suffering. For the scientists among you, Buddhist teacher Shinzen Young says, $S = P \times R$. Suffering equals pain times resistance.[13]

All of these stories we have told ourselves and believed have been triggers for us to act out, become angry, and/or binge on alcohol, food, drugs, porn, gambling, codependent behaviors, sex, overwork, love, gaming. The list is endless.

Expectations will get us into trouble. They will be the cause of our suffering. When we expect something to happen and it doesn't happen, we are upset, we tell ourselves we have been let down, and we are disappointed and angry.

We create the dramas in our lives with our thinking. As I mentioned above, I used to think that we were powerless over our thoughts. However, we can have some effect on them. For example, if I have the thought, *I am not good enough*, it can affect the next moment of me deciding not to do something.

If we witnessed an accident, our thinking would be impacted in the next moment – we would be concerned whether the person or people were okay. There is nothing wrong with thought or thinking. The mind/

heart produces thought, and we need thinking to be able to survive this world. However, we can learn a different and more productive way of engaging with thought.

Thought will arise, and we don't have to identify with it, fix it, solidify it. Thought is often not fact. Thought and thinking are often interpretations and perceptions about something or someone. They are just views. A magic trick. An illusion. Have you ever fallen in lust or in love with someone, and months later can't believe what it was that attracted you to this person? What attracted you was the narrative you created in your head – you fell in lust and/or love with the illusion you created.

By the time we are in a story, we are so caught up in the seductive cycle of thinking that it becomes challenging to break the cycle. While it may be possible to step off, our chances are reduced considerably.

We all love a good story, and the stories we tell ourselves are the best. These stories give us permission to continue using our choice of distraction and substances. They can convince us that we don't have issues, that we don't have compulsive behaviors or addictions. They make excuses about why we can't stop or why we need to continue. They mask pain, and emotions, we don't want to experience.

ONE-MINUTE REFLECTION

EGO: Energy Gone Overboard. Reflect on the energy you feel in the body right now. Has it gone overboard so much that it is impacting on how you are thinking?

FIVE-MINUTE REFLECTION

E *Ease the body into a comfortable position.*

G *Generate kindness toward your thoughts and thinking by saying:* Today I ask you to relax so

I can have some peace. Come and go as you wish, but I'm not going to be listening to your every word.

0 *Open up to new possibilities. Open up to doing something different, by not listening to the thinking, by asking the thinking to step back. Open up to the possibility of retiring the thinking that causes anxiety and distress.*

TWENTY-MINUTE REFLECTION

What do our stories give us permission to do?

- They continue to remind me of my past.
- They stop me from letting go of my past.
- They can convince me I don't have addictions.
- They can give me permission to continue using my choice of distractions.
- They make excuses about why I need to continue holding on to my habits.
- They mask my pain and emotions so I don't have to experience feelings.

Now include some of your own reflections.

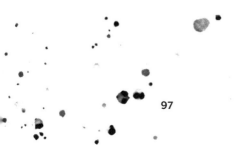

YOUR OWN
REFLECTIONS

~

- _____
  _____
- _____
  _____
- _____
  _____
- _____
  _____
- _____
  _____

A BREATH OF FRESH AIR

In our closing reflection, we will face our thinking with our breath. And learn to become comfortable with the uncomfortable.

Whenever we notice that we are experiencing bodily pain or difficult emotions, as best we can, we try to face the pain just as it is and let go of any stories we are telling ourselves about the pain.

Begin by settling into a comfortable posture, bringing your attention onto your breath and following your breath as it moves in and out of the body. Then, whenever you notice a painful sensation, as best you can, recognize the difference between the raw primary painful sensations and the responses of aversion toward it.

If the pain is emotional, notice the difference between the raw emotion and the thoughts about it – the stories or narrative you tell yourself about it. As best you can, allow the primary painful sensations to be there.

Breathe into the sensations. If the pain is mainly emotional, there will be physical sensations associated with the emotion – breathe into these bodily sensations, with a sense of friendliness and curiosity.

As best you can, let go of the stories about the pain; open to and feel into the raw sensations. If the sensations are very strong, breathe onto the edge of the area where the sensations feel intense. If it's helpful, say to yourself, *It's okay, it's already here, let me feel it.*

Now close this booklet, allow yourself to pause, and remember to breathe with ease.

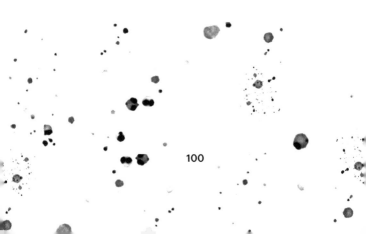

Actions are like the wind:
just as the wind blows us around,
our actions blow us and others around too.

8

ACTIONS
HAVE
CONSEQUENCES

INSIDE THE KIT
Smelling salts

Smell flowers, the fresh air – shake yourself out of the "poor me" state.

IN AN EMERGENCY
Ask for help

Ask for help. Even the Buddha asked for help! When he was assailed by doubt, he touched the earth and asked the earth goddess to be his witness.

TIP

Mother earth is always there to support us. Remember this right now as you feel the gravity of the earth supporting you to be here, now.

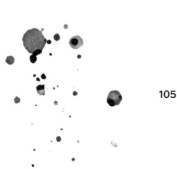

Turning away creates a replay

Actions have consequences. There are four habitual
unhelpful actions we take when dealing with mental
and physical pain:

- we avoid and are annoyed;
- we blame and shame others;
- we blame and call ourselves names;
- we fall into self-pity and listen to our internal
  committee.

All of them may actually protect us in the short term.
In the long term, the consequences can make it much
harder for us to cultivate more freedom in our lives.

Distracting behavior is one way to avoid pain. When
something difficult shows up, we reach for the phone,
the flat screen, or Netflix, have a drink, eat some candy,
reach for something external like sex or gambling, or
take a substance. Many of us try to brutally eradicate our
thoughts and feelings with our choice of self-medication.
And guess what? The feelings and thoughts just bounce
back again once the self-medication has worn off.

Yes, we can distract ourselves from difficult situations with some healthier habits like calling a friend to have a good laugh about trivial things, or going for a walk, sitting in nature. While distractions can be helpful, we have to remember at some point that we do have to come back to the thing we have been avoiding, otherwise it will begin to plague the mind.

Blaming others is something we have all done in our lives. When you can't find your phone or your keys, who do you blame? If you are anything like me, you will blame the kids, or your partner, or even the dog. And those of you who live alone blame the person who visited you a month ago.

Laughable, but, the next time you lose something, become aware of the unpleasant feeling tone in the body, and how you want to move away from it by blaming, which can of course trigger anger, frustration, and at worse a relapse in someone's recovery.

When we blame others, we are trying our best to take control of an uncomfortable situation, and avoid being in touch with any upset or sadness that may arise. Blaming others means we don't have to take any responsibility for our actions. However, the consequence is that others will be upset and angry with us. It pushes down our emotions, and gets rid of any thoughts of being out of control. Sometimes blame also protects an unrealistic image or idea of ourselves as perfect.

If adults or siblings always blamed us for things going wrong in our childhood, self-blame can become a trauma response. It can protect us, while at the same time it makes us small. Our response becomes all about us and can often lead to self-pity.

In my book *Eight Step Recovery: Using the Buddha's Teachings to Overcome Addiction*, I talk about hating myself with a vengeance. Sometimes I even enjoyed saying *I hate myself*; it was as if it gave me some kind of power. It also gave me an excuse not to do anything about my life – I was that person who kept on going down the same road, and falling down the same hole. I would drag myself out of the hole, and proceed to walk down the same road and fall down the same dark hole.

My self-hatred often turned into self-pity. As I mentioned earlier, I used to think that the only way out of my suffering was to take my life. I thought something was desperately wrong with me because I was experiencing so much emotional distress that I couldn't understand. I told myself I had a happy childhood, and so to be miserable and depressed was not allowed. Little did I know I was holding on to the few happy moments in my childhood so I wouldn't become emotionally disturbed. For many years, I assumed I was the only person in the world who was suffering and in turmoil, and nobody could understand me. Self-pity did soothe me to an extent; however, it meant I did very little to help myself out of the painful rut. In fact, there was a part of me that wanted to hide behind the self-pity. I wanted people to notice something was wrong with me, I wanted people to see my pain. Nobody ever did, which gave me more permission to dwell in my self-pity.

When I came across the Buddha's first noble truth – that, because of the human condition of sickness, aging, and death, there would be suffering in my life – it was like a thunderbolt. Overnight I became normal. I realized that many people around me must be suffering, and that suffering is a part of life that cannot be avoided. This truth was an invitation to stop beating myself up about how something was drastically wrong with me, and begin to explore what had happened to me.

Because I was someone who used to blame, distract, go into self-pity or self-hatred, I could really see how my actions had consequences. Consequences that were often harmful to me, rather than helpful in my life.

I used to tell myself that I achieved much better out of chaos, to the extent that, when things were going well, I would intentionally do something to sabotage them. I would pick an argument with my partner, or let my personal space become a mess filled with clutter, or go on a binge. This thinking came from the fact that, in childhood, I had a choice to either survive the mayhem or be sedated. In one children's home I was in, the cook was often found in the early morning slumped in front of the fridge due to alcoholism. Together with some staff, we had to make the breakfast. Once we had sat down to eat, some of the kids would be so angry they would turn over the tables and chairs, or start screaming all day. Those kids who were having a normal reaction of anger and distress to the abnormal situation of finding our cook passed out, sometimes thinking she was dead, were medicated and/or sent to an institution.

So I learned to ride the bedlam silently and be the perfect child. Twenty years later, I was creating my own disarray, and the reward was the completion of a project. The cost meant sometimes I'd lose myself in the chaos, and sometimes I put myself at risk. When things were going well, it was scary and I would panic. I didn't know how to be with nothing much going on. It felt weird in my body, and I would be on tenterhooks waiting for something to go wrong. So I'd create the chaos to give me a false sense of safety.

And yet I kept on acting out. Does this sound familiar? Creating chaos may not be your source of sabotage, but many people have habits that get in the way of their freedom, and keep them stuck on the cycle. I could not accept that my actions were having a detrimental impact on me. So, let's take a more universal look at our actions.

What is your story?

As we saw in the last chapter, the cycle is not linear. Our actions of anger, resentment, addictive and compulsive behaviors are often triggered by moving away from pain, which then becomes emotions and stinking thinking.

KISSING THE EARTH

ONE-MINUTE REFLECTION

Today I share a gift from the grandmothers. We can do this in our home or outside in the garden or a park.

Find a good place to lie face down, with your navel exposed to the earth or the floor. And have the sense of your navel kissing the earth or the floor you lie upon.

As you breathe in, say, *I know I am breathing in*.

As you breathe out, say, *I know I am breathing out*.

And now have the feeling of you drinking in the energy of the earth as you breathe in, and, as you exhale, let go of any distress that the body held on to during its birth.

And surrender: just lie and be supported by the earth – the floor that comes from the earth.

FIVE-MINUTE REFLECTION

As you lie face down, have your navel exposed to the earth, or the floor. And have the sense of your naval kissing the earth or the floor you lie upon.

Breathe in – *I know I am breathing in*.

Breathe out – *I know I am breathing out*.

And now have the feeling of you drinking in the energy of the earth as you breathe in, and, as you exhale, let go of any distress that the body held on to during its birth.

Breathe in – *I know I am breathing in*.

Breathe out – *I know I am breathing out*.

And now have the feeling of you drinking in the energy of the earth as you breathe in, and, as you exhale,

let go of any distress that the body held on to during your childhood.

Breathe in – *I know I am breathing in*.

Breathe out – *I know I am breathing out*.

And now have the feeling of you drinking in the energy of the earth as you breathe in, and, as you exhale, let go of any distress that the body held on to during your adolescence.

Breathe in – *I know I am breathing in*.

Breathe out – *I know I am breathing out*.

Surrender to the earth: roll over and just allow yourself to gaze upward to the sky or to the ceiling – and relax.

I hope this short practice will nourish you. And fill you with all the energy that you need. May you walk gently on the earth today. May you breathe in the air with gratitude today. May you drink clean water with thanks today. May you feel into the warmth of your body today.

TWENTY-MINUTE REFLECTION

Lie on your back, surrender to the earth or the floor, and just gaze up with no agenda. Just allow yourself to do nothing for twenty minutes.

Breaking the cycle is like surfing
the waves: take risks, be carried
by unseen forces.

9

BREAKING THE CYCLE

INSIDE THE KIT
Epipen

When all else fails, call on your ancestors. Ask them: what would they do to heal the heart/mind? Our ancestors have our back and can help reduce the overwhelming anxiety we have been holding on to. There are biological ancestors who may be supportive – but sometimes these ancestors need to be quarantined. If this is the case, call on affinity ancestors, people who have inspired you and have passed over to the other side. Remember, we are our ancestors' wildest dream. The life each of us is living now is so different from the life our ancestors lived a hundred years ago. We live this life now because of their wisdom.

IN AN EMERGENCY
Pray

Get down on your knees and pray to your God, to Buddha, Allah, Nature, or your Higher Power. Chant mantras, sing songs. Do something different.

TIP

When I lived in Arnhem Land, the Australian Aborigines gave me this teaching: always look beyond the fire, because if you look into the fire it will send you psychotic. This fire can be a metaphor for the mind full of feelings, thoughts, and emotions, and, if we look directly into the mind, it will send us insane too. We need to learn to look beyond the mind for our freedom.

119

An end of the struggle

Many people are searching for enlightenment, looking for the god moments. There is nothing wrong with this desire, but what it means is we can spiritually bypass, and stay a prisoner of our minds. It means that we can ignore all the difficult situations in our lives, if we constantly turn away from unpleasant experience by pushing away or distracting. We are also not satisfied with pleasant experience because we don't want it to end, and when it ends we are disappointed, we get upset, or we wish it could be better. The problem is that what we often resist persists.

Today I can still slip into wishing my experience was better. I can be out on a warm summer's day, walking in the woods near me, hearing the song of the birds and the soothing sound of a waterfall. I sit down to drink in this beautiful moment and a voice in my head says, *Wouldn't it be great to have a glass of champagne and a spliff?* I chuckle because I know in that moment I am moving away from a pleasant experience and chasing after bliss, enlightenment.

Before he woke up to seeing things as they really are and became awake as a Buddha, the Prince didn't vow to attain enlightenment – he vowed to find an end of suffering. In waking up to the truth, the Prince had to turn toward strong mental states that arose in his mind. He thought that someone was trying to kill him with arrows; he was assailed with lust, sense desire, boredom, ill will, and doubt. At no point did he identify with these emotional states, or go into proliferation of thought. And when doubt arose strongly in his mind – as a voice in his mind asking, *Who gives you the right to the seat of enlightenment?* – he asked for help.

This allegory of the Prince becoming enlightened points to the fact that, if we want freedom, if we want the heart/mind to be one, we have to face all experience without identifying with it or running away from it. We have to let go of the struggle.

However, it is important to remember several things:

• We push things away for a reason.
• Our distractions, our addictive and compulsive behaviors, our outbursts of aggression, our trauma responses of withdrawal, fawning – they all have a function.
• Nothing is wrong with you. The question to reflect on is, *What happened to you?* It's so much easier to say something is wrong with us, when in fact society has labelled us. And, when we hold that story,

we don't have to face what happened to us.

- Our behaviors that may be categorized as abnormal are in fact normal for us. In the words of a friend and teacher, Dr. Gabor Maté, our adaptive behaviors "are a normal response to abnormal situations."

For example, I have often been labelled as intimidating, growing up in a white environment experiencing racism daily at school, and in the home. For my survival, I had to become assertive, become big.

I have known obese people who have said they are big to protect themselves from ever being physically or sexually abused again. Their obesity is a normal response to abnormal behaviors of sexual and physical assault in childhood.

Understanding what we gain from our adaptive behaviors can help us cultivate self-compassion. The fact is that our addictions and compulsive behaviors are what Dr. Gabor Maté calls "adaptations to trauma in our childhood." We hold on to our addictive and compulsive behaviors for a reason.

"Where there is pain, there is gain." Why do we say this? Well, there is no reason to change if we're always feeling pleasant. The reality is that, if we respond differently to our triggers, we will experience pain, but in the next breath we will find a new freedom. Let discomfort become your teacher, and, when in pain, ask for help.

So, while we think we may only gain something from our trauma responses that keep us separate and other, we can also gain something in letting go of these responses, and coming into relationship with feelings that have been overwhelming us. Remember we are not alone – I do not know anybody who has never struggled. When we become aware of the collective suffering, rather than thinking, *This is my suffering and I am the only person who is suffering*, we can have a sense of community supporting us and holding us.

Struggling with an addiction or compulsive habitual behavior

It's a human tendency to find fault or difficulty in something when we haven't fully committed to change. If we are here because we have been struggling with a habitual behavior or an addiction, to pause when we have been activated or afflicted by overwhelming and unhelpful thinking will admittedly be challenging, especially when the four C's of addiction are in play: craving, compulsion to use, loss of control, continuing to use despite the negative consequences.

There is the strong magnetic craving to pick up our choice of distraction when something has upset us, or when we fear an enjoyable time ending. Already activated, we can be out in the world and our eye catches sight of a bottle of wine, or a porn magazine, or a cream cake. We salivate, butterflies begin to flutter in our stomach, and a strong compulsion to pick up arises in our experience. Excitement arises, and we begin to have memories and stories of our intoxicated past. At this point, we don't want to stop: we are having fun in our heads. We gain some moments of pleasure. At this point, we lose control, pick up, and continue to use despite the negative consequences. What's the point of changing? We have gained a pleasurable experience for a few minutes.

We can also be triggered by a text message or an email, which can activate unpleasant sensations in the body. We are thrown off-centre and automatically respond without thinking. And, before we know it, we are in a conflict, and we are either unfriended or we unfriend someone on Facebook.

Addictive, compulsive, and habitual behaviors do serve a purpose. Some people will tell you that they became an alcoholic or addicted to drugs because they were extremely shy. Aged fourteen or fifteen, they were invited to their first party and offered a joint, a line of coke, or a glass of wine. And their whole world changed in seconds. They were no longer socially awkward – they became the clown of the party, confident, and their self-esteem was enhanced. They found the answer to their problem. Alcohol and drugs became their doorway into a new exciting life. Others develop a fantasy world or compulsive thinking to escape their childhood reality.

Once we have tried the substance or engaged in the behavior, we return to it for certain reasons. We want to enjoy the high again, or we want to be part of the in-crowd. Maybe we drink because it makes it easier to socialize. Perhaps control of our food intake helps us to feel more self-confident, or heroin helps us to forget all our worries.

We may have grown up in homes where the abuse of alcohol, illegal or pharmaceutical drugs, food, or money was the norm, and so it may seem normal for us as adults too. As the addiction takes hold, these reasons may change. In the end, it may be just that our behavior relieves withdrawal symptoms, and we don't feel we could live any other way. Nevertheless, whatever our habits, there is something that we get from our behavior.

It can be so easy to beat ourselves up in the aftermath of a binge, a slip, or a relapse. These are behaviors that have protected us and helped us survive.

For some people, addiction has been a way of self-medicating, and has become a habit of misguided self-compassion. The gain here is that we have the desire to take care of ourselves, the desire to make things better. It's just that we need to find a different way to lessen the many risks that come with the addictive and compulsive lifestyle.

We also hear many people, in the rooms of Twelve Steps, Refuge Recovery, Smart Recovery, Eight Step Recovery, say that their addiction has brought them to a place with the divine. If it wasn't for their addiction, they may never have found God, Allah, Buddha, and/or mindfulness. They may never have opened up the Bible, the Koran, the *Bhagavad Gita*, the *Dhammapada*, the "Big Book" of Alcoholics Anonymous, or other inspiring texts. And this is what has helped them to become abstinent and have more sobriety of mind. It is possible to slow the cycle down and step off.

For some people, their anxiety, depression, anger, or aggression has brought them to therapy or to psychedelic-assisted therapy, which has transformed their life.

Compassion in action

When we bring kindness and compassion to our pain, it is not to let ourselves off the hook for what we have done, or to gloss over or to make it okay that we have hurt others. We may well feel regret, but beating ourselves up is not going to help. Bringing compassion to what we have done allows us to accept what has happened, rather than flee from it.

Letting go of our reactivity our adaptive behaviors stands between us and recovery. The pain of the costs of our adaptive behaviors also stands between us and our recovery, and makes it harder to let go. It is like saying goodbye to a friend. It can feel like

a bereavement. The pain of letting go is the grief that
we can be scared to experience. What will soothe
us now? What will keep the messy feelings at bay?

The alcohol, the food, the messy emotions, and the habits
are the reason why we need a first aid kit, so what now?

To let go means we have to change. Facing the pain in
our lives, including the pain of the costs of our adaptive
behaviors, can seem insurmountable. We Fear Everything
And Run (FEAR), we believe False Evidence Appearing
Real (FEAR). Fear immobilizes us, and many of us just
bury our head under the comforter, and hope for the best.
Unable to face the pain of letting go, we automatically
turn toward our choice of distraction to alleviate the pain.
And we are back on the vicious cycle of thinking without
even realizing what we are doing. We are unaware
because we have been avoiding pain for many years,
because we think that not feeling is the answer to our
troubles. Or because we think that, if we allow ourselves
to stop and feel, we will collapse and never be able to
get out of bed in the morning and live our lives.

One day, we do have to become compassionate toward
ourselves. We do have to face the reality of what is
happening in our lives. We have to learn to accept
ourselves, and that means liking ourselves, forgiving

ourselves, being patient with ourselves, and being kind toward ourselves.

For some of us, the cost of our reactivity and compulsive behaviors may be terrifying. Some people have lost their home and family. Some people are living with a life-threatening illness; some people have been disabled by their behaviors. Some of us may have been sent to prison. With kindness, we have to learn to accept some of these painful costs. We cannot change the past, but we can learn to relate to the past differently by learning to love and forgive ourselves right now.

There may be people who are angry toward us, people who are negative toward us. Not everyone will accept an apology. If we can forgive ourselves, it won't be so traumatic if others don't forgive us.

We may even think, because we're not being triggered anymore, just stuck in the stage of actions and consequences, that life is better. But the only way to interrupt the cycle is to feel the pain in the body. And that means learning to be kind and gentle with ourselves. That means giving ourselves a hug when we slip, and knowing in the next moment we can pick ourselves back up to do something different in the next breath.

Compassion in action is when we can feel the sadness and the pain of not being able to change the past, and we are able to make new choices in the now. If we dwell only in the sadness and remorse, we are likely to become immobilized and stuck on the cycle. For example, I had to feel the sadness and loss of my teeth crumbling; when I could face this cost of my addiction with an open heart, I was able to act differently. I had my teeth repaired, and I began to let go of my addiction. For several years, I had walked around with damaged front teeth because I had inadvertently become consumed by self-pity.

There are never endings – only
separations and new beginnings.

10

WHAT NEXT?

The alchemy is in the now, and trusting that, if we change in this moment, it will impact the next. For example, if we have picked up our choice of distraction, we could interrupt this by breathing into the body and in the next moment put it back down, and in the next moment ask for help, and in the next moment move ourselves away from the conditions that activated us, and in the next moment take a breath and stop.

Where there is loss, there will be gain if we are patient, if we allow the law of cause and effect to take its natural time. Where there is pleasure, there is pain. Where there is praise there is blame. And where there is fame there is disrepute. This is the Buddha's teaching of the eight worldly winds, reminding us that everything changes, and, when we can accept this, the mind/heart will find some freedom and peace.

What happens when nothing you have tried has worked, and you are still in conflict with your mind? What next? Have you tried all the things in the first aid kit? Is there just one thing that can help soothe the mind? The answer may be no, not at all – that is progress to recognize something is not working. It may mean you need the Jaws of Life! Something to pull you out of your toxic situation. Which could mean seeking intensive therapy, booking yourself into rehab, taking medication, seeking out other alternatives.

INSIDE THE KIT
Jaws of life

If all else fails, book yourself into rehab, book yourself some intensive therapy, try Emotional Freedom Technique (EFT) tapping, consider taking prescribed medication. If you are fortunate enough to live in a country where ketamine, psilocybin, or MDMA-assisted therapy is legal, this may be your calling too.

IN AN EMERGENCY
Don't give up

TIP

Reflect on your ethical life.

One of my teachers, the late Urgyen Sangharakshita, said, if our mind is caught in turmoil, or if we are experiencing a lot of conflict in our lives, we should reflect on our ethical life. Below are the eight steps in Buddhist recovery, to help us do exactly this.

Eight steps toward emotional and mental sobriety

- STEP ONE: accepting that this human life will bring suffering.[14]
- STEP TWO: seeing how we create extra suffering in our lives.
- STEP THREE: embracing impermanence to show us that our suffering can end.
- STEP FOUR: being willing to step onto the path of recovery and discover freedom.
- STEP FIVE: transforming our speech, actions, and livelihood.
- STEP SIX: placing positive values at the center of our lives.
- STEP SEVEN: making every effort to stay on the path of recovery.
- STEP EIGHT: helping others by sharing the benefits we have gained.

You have arrived here, either by reading through the whole book, or by flipping to the end. Pause, turn inward, and ask yourself: *Why am I here? Has this been of help? Is there something I am looking for, and still haven't found?* I encourage you to let go of what you think it is you need, and be open to something that is revealed to you on these pages. You may be surprised.

KINDNESS

A LAST ONE-MINUTE REFLECTION

Give yourself kindness. Touch a hand upon your heart and feel the warmth of your own hand. Know that this is you giving and receiving kindness toward yourself.

Take three deep breaths. Purse your lips into a tight hole as if you were sucking on a straw, and then take three deep breaths in filling your whole body.

In and out

In and out

In and out

Now close this book, open up your stance like you belong in the world, and take up space with the length and width of your body, standing, sitting, walking, or lying down with dignity and pride. You are loved, you belong here in the world.

NOTES AND REFERENCES

1   See https://www.nicabm.com/trauma-how-to-help-your-
    clients-understand-their-window-of-tolerance/, accessed
    on November 16, 2023.

2   Patrick Carnes, *A Gentle Path through the Twelve Steps: The
    Classic Guide for All People in the Process of Recovery*, Hazelden,
    Center City, MN, 2012, p.12.

3   In *The Foundations of Mindfulness or Satipatthana Sutta,* the
    Buddha teaches contemplation of the body, feelings, states
    of mind, and *dhammas* or phenomena, which together
    are referred to as the "four foundations." See https://www.
    accesstoinsight.org/lib/authors/nyanasatta/wheel019.html,
    accessed on November 16, 2023.

4   The Buddha's teachings on each of the four foundations of
    mindfulness are arranged into tetrads, or sets of four
    instructions. The first tetrad contains four instructions relating
    to the body.

5   *The Ball of Honey or Madhupindika Sutta* (MN 18), available at
    http://www.accesstoinsight.org/tipitaka/mn/mn.018.than.html,
    accessed on November 16, 2023.

6   Pema Chödrön, *The Places That Scare You*, HarperCollins,
    London 2004, p.75.

7   Valerie Mason-John and Paramabandhu Groves, *Eight Step
    Recovery: Using the Buddha's Teachings to Overcome Addiction*,
    Windhorse Publications, Cambridge 2018, p.289.

8   Mason-John and Groves, *Eight Step Recovery*, p.xxxvi.

9   See https://www.6seconds.org/2022/03/13/plutchik-wheel-
    emotions/, accessed on November 16, 2023.

10 Mason-John and Groves, *Eight Step Recovery*, p.46.

11 This is a gender-neutral rendering based on the translation at https://www.dhammatalks.org/suttas/MN/MN20.html, accessed on November 16, 2023.

12 The founder of IFS, Richard Schwartz, says, "IFS offers an effective alternative to the restraining, managerial approach of the *Vitakkasanthana Sutta*." He suggests that these thoughts are coming from protective parts of you that need to be loved and comforted rather than restrained or redirected.

13 See https://angelabeeching.com/s-p-x-r-explains-why-we-may-be-stuck-or-feeling-powerless/, accessed on November 16, 2023.

14 Mason-John and Groves, *Eight Step Recovery*, p.i.

WINDHORSE PUBLICATIONS

Windhorse Publications is a Buddhist charitable company based in the United Kingdom. We place great emphasis on producing books of high quality that are accessible and relevant to those interested in Buddhism at whatever level. We are the main publisher of the works of Sangharakshita, the founder of the Triratna Buddhist Order and Community. Our books draw on the whole range of the Buddhist tradition, including translations of traditional texts, commentaries, books that make links with contemporary culture and ways of life, biographies of Buddhists, and works on meditation.

As a not-for-profit enterprise, we ensure that all surplus income is invested in new books and improved production methods, to better communicate Buddhism in the twenty-first century. We welcome donations to help us continue our work – to find out more, go to windhorsepublications.com.

The Windhorse is a mythical animal that flies over the earth carrying on its back three precious jewels, bringing these invaluable gifts to all humanity: the Buddha (the "Awakened One"), his teaching, and the community of all his followers.

Windhorse Publications
38 Newmarket Road
Cambridge CB5 8DT – UK
info@windhorsepublications.com

Consortium Book Sales & Distribution
210 American Drive
Jackson TN 38301 – USA

Windhorse Books
PO Box 574
Newtown NSW 2042 – Australia

THE TRIRATNA BUDDHIST COMMUNITY

Windhorse Publications is a part of the Triratna Buddhist
Community, an international movement with centres in Europe,
India, North and South America, and Australasia. At these centres,
members of the Triratna Buddhist Order offer classes in meditation
and Buddhism. Activities of the Triratna Community also include
retreat centres, residential spiritual communities, ethical Right
Livelihood businesses, and the Karuna Trust, a United Kingdom
fundraising charity that supports social welfare projects in the
slums and villages of India.

Through these and other activities, Triratna is developing a
unique approach to Buddhism, not simply as a philosophy and
a set of techniques, but as a creatively directed way of life for all
people living in the conditions of the modern world.

If you would like more information about Triratna please visit
thebuddhistcentre.com or write to:

London Buddhist Centre
51 Roman Road
London E2 0HU – UK
contact@lbc.org.uk

Aryaloka
14 Heartwood Circle
Newmarket NH 03857 – USA
info@aryaloka.org

Sydney Buddhist Centre
24 Enmore Road
Sydney NSW 2042 – Australia
info@sydneybuddhistcentre.org.au

EIGHT STEP RECOVERY: USING THE BUDDHA'S TEACHINGS TO OVERCOME ADDICTION

Valerie Mason-John and Dr. Paramabandhu Groves

Human nature has an inbuilt tendency towards addiction. All of us can struggle with this tendency, but for some it can destroy their lives. Fortunately, recovery is widespread too. What can the Buddha's teachings offer us in our recovery from addiction? They offer an understanding of how the mind works, tools for helping a mind vulnerable to addiction, and ways to overcome addictive and obsessive behaviour, cultivating a calm, clear mind without anger and resentments.

'Through Buddhist teachings, personal experiences, and case examples, this book provides a wise illustration of the fundamental processes underlying a broad range of addictive behaviors. Mason-John and Groves offer here a practical and compassionate step-by-step guide to freedom from the deep trappings and suffering of addiction.' – **Sarah Bowen**, Assistant Professor, Department of Psychiatry and Behavioral Sciences, University of Washington, author of *Mindfulness-Based Relapse Prevention for Addictive Behaviors: A Clinician's Guide*

'Blending the MBAR program with traditional Buddhist teachings and personal stories, the authors give us a wise and compassionate approach to recovery from the range of addictions. This comprehensive approach will be a valuable tool for addicts and addiction professionals alike.' – **Kevin Griffin**, author of *One Breath at a Time: Buddhism and the Twelve Steps*

'The eight steps outlined here provide a simple, wise, and practical approach to recovery from a wide range of compulsive patterns of behaviour associated with suffering. They provide a spiritual pathway to recovery for people from any faith tradition, as well as for those who are not religious, and for those who suffer from addiction as well as those who are simply aware of the suffering associated with the human condition. This is a book for everyone!' – **Professor Chris Cook**, Director of the Project for Spirituality, Theology & Health, Durham University

ISBN 978-1-911407-12-6
360 pages

Printed in the USA
CPSIA information can be obtained
at www.ICGtesting.com
LVHW061143280424
778681LV00010B/131

9 781915 342232